Men of Property

An analysis of the Norwich enrolled deeds 1285-1311

by

Serena Kelly

Elizabeth Rutledge

Margot Tillyard

edited by

Ursula Priestley

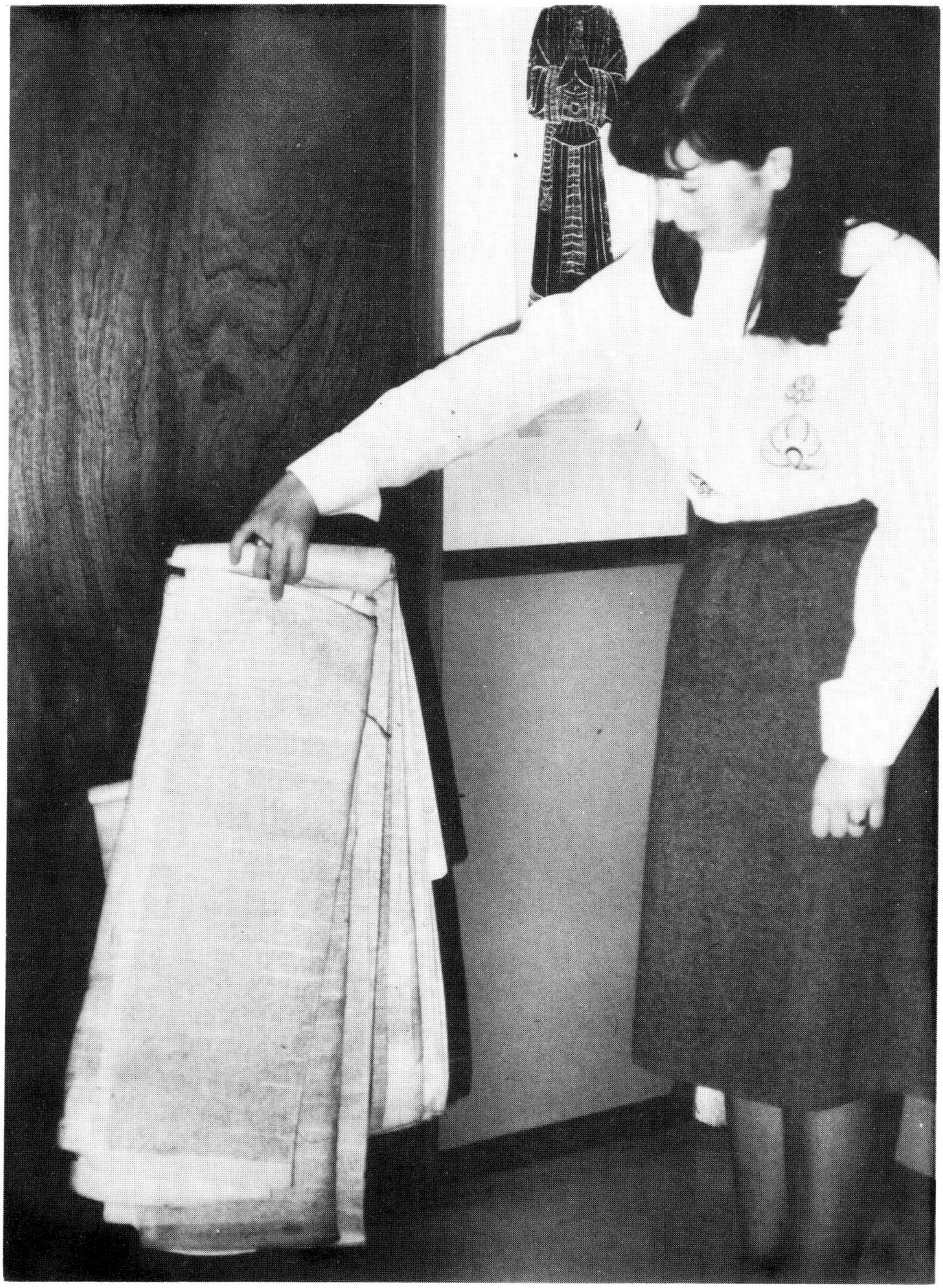

Helen Sutermeister holding one of the early Norwich court rolls on which this booklet is based.

CONTENTS

ILLUSTRATIONS

INTRODUCTION

by

Alan Carter

The Norwich Survey, of which a short general account has recently been published,[1] was established in 1971 with the intention that it should undertake a joint archaeological and historical investigation of the origins and development of the City. As ever, more interest was shown in funding the digging of holes than the reading of documents, and so the initial historical research of the Survey, characterized by the Pottergate report of 1974, was done on an entirely voluntary and part-time basis. Despite the fact that that report[2] showed the full potential of the evidence it was not for another two years that funding for full-time documentary investigation was obtained, this with the generous financial support of the Department of the Environment. The Oak Street report[3] of 1978 represented the first fruit of what was then intended as a systematic programme of research into the voluminous records of the medieval and post-medieval city[4] but sadly, even then, it was known that Helen Sutermeister, the originator and inspiration of the project, had incurable cancer. In May 1979, her work unfinished, she died aged only 36, and her colleagues and research assistants were faced with the task of trying to bring her work to completion. To do so in its entirety would have been impossible: it was decided, instead, to concentrate on two critical aspects of her work, the investigation of the early deed evidence (with which this booklet is concerned) and the analysis of later probate inventories (now published in the journal Post-Medieval Archaeology).[5]

The investigation of the deeds was always seen as a means to producing a complete register of medieval property ownership within the walls of Norwich.[6] Such a directory would have been of enormous value to both archaeologists, historians and to students of domestic and ecclesiastical architecture. It would have, and has,[7] enabled the archaeologists not only to choose their sites sensibly (for less than one in ten of all developments can be excavated) but also to interpret better what they found.[8] The historian would be provided with an invaluable tool for the investigation of the economic and social topography of the City (such as is attempted below, pp.13-39), while the architectural historians would have been able to trace the tenure of the buildings they were studying. In the event, that register was not completed. To have done so would have meant widening the scope of the enquiry to incorporate the evidence of sources other than the deeds, and in the time available this was simply not possible. A decision was taken, instead, to concentrate on the period between 1285 and 1340 (after which there is a long gap in the records[9]) and to analyse this evidence in two ways. The first, which is exemplified in Margot Tillyard's paper below (pp.5-11) was the reconstruction of the city's topography and the pattern of property ownership. The end result was a series of coloured manuscript plans (now deposited in the Norfolk Record Office[10]) covering the whole area of the city other than the exempt jurisdiction[11] of the Castle and Priory fees (Fig.3). The second line of enquiry involved the computerization of the details recorded in the deeds, and the tabulation, analysis and mapping of this data in an examination of the economic and trade structure of the city. Here, even before Helen Sutermeister's death, it was apparent that the bulk of the material could easily overwhelm the project and so an end date of 1311 was adopted. The evidence was not always susceptible to interpretation, and the biggest problem was that only just over a quarter of the individuals named in the deeds could be included in the analysis. The final figures, therefore, are small, but despite this and despite the problem of not being able to say with certainty whether a person of a named trade lived where they owned property,[12] a fascinating and convincing picture has emerged of the economy and the economic topography of the medieval city (Fig.5).

As the work by Margot Tillyard and Serena Kelly proceeded, more and more questions about the nature and reliability of the evidence began to suggest themselves. It was decided that the best way of answering these was to invite a legal historian, Elizabeth Rutledge, to join the team. Her paper, then, begins with an examination of the nature of enrolment and of the documents enrolled to see whether and to what extent this might affect work based on the deeds. Her second concern was to discover what changes, if any, occurred in property interests in Norwich and for convenience the period she took was again that of the first five rolls - 1285 to 1311. Her conclusions were not at all what one might have expected and perhaps the most interesting of them concerns the way in which married women compliantly divested themselves of their rights to property after a codification of Norwich property law in the years around 1306.

The material in these three very different papers is not always easy to approach, and nowhere is this more obvious than in the section on the basis of calculations in Serena Kelly's work. Here, however, as with the technical vocabulary necessary in Elizabeth Rutledge's text, a little patience will be rewarded, for what might initially appear rather difficult will rapidly become clear. It was thought that the best way of introducing the reader to the material was to start with the shortest and least intricate discussion, and to move on from this to matter that became increasingly complex. The one disadvantage that this presents is that it is not until the final paper that the reader is offered critical comment on the nature of enrolment and of the documents enrolled: both matters that have a close bearing on the interpretations put forward in the first two papers. It is hoped, though, that, with their interests whetted and their curiosity aroused, readers will wish to move backwards and forwards through what we hope are adequately signposted (or sub-headed) texts.

ACKNOWLEDGEMENTS

The authors wish to record their grateful thanks to Miss J.M. Kennedy, County Archivist, for permission to reproduce documents in her custody and to the staff of the Norfolk Record Office for the long-continued assistance and generous encouragement. Acknowledgement is due also to those other volunteer assistants, notably Alayne Fenner, who worked with Margot Tillyard on the reconstruction maps. Dr Derek Keene gave unstintingly of his time in commenting on successive drafts of the three papers; the authors all benefitted from his criticism, but such errors or infelicities as remain are their responsibility alone. The drawings are by Phillip Judge and the photographs of the deeds by Michael Brandon-Jones. Typing was by Mavis Bithray and Frances Randell.

The papers are published with the help of a large grant from the Helen Sutermeister Memorial Fund, and we are grateful to all those who supported the appeal that established this.

Much of the original research was funded by the Department of the Environment; further generous grants towards its completion were made by the Alderman Norman Foundation and by Anglia Television. Without their support the work would have been impossible, and we are deeply grateful to them.

ENDNOTES

1. Norwich Survey, The Norwich Survey 1971-1980, 2nd edition (Norwich 1980).

2. A. Carter, J.P. Roberts and H. Sutermeister, 'Excavations in Norwich - 1973. The Norwich Survey - Third Interim Report', Norfolk Archaeology XXXVI, 1974, pp.50-4.

3. M.W. Atkin and H. Sutermeister, 'Excavations in Norwich - 1977/78. The Norwich Survey - Seventh Interim Report', Norfolk Archaeology XXXVII, 1978, pp.35-44.

4. As envisaged in A. Carter, 'Sampling in a medieval town: the study of Norwich' in J.F. Cherry, C. Gamble and S. Shennan (eds.), Sampling in Contemporary British Archaeology (BAR British Series 50, Oxford 1978) especially pp.271-6.

5. Ursula Priestley and P.J. Corfield, 'Rooms and room use in Norwich housing, 1580-1730', Post-Medieval Archaeology 16, 1982, pp.93-123.

6. With the exception of a small suburb at Heigham the built-up area lay almost entirely within the late-13th-century walls; see W. Hudson and J.C. Tingey (eds.), The Records of the City of Norwich I (Norwich 1906) pp. lxxix-lxxx and J. Campbell, Norwich (fascicle of the Historic Town Plans Atlas, London 1975) p.23.

7. On this see Carter 'Sampling ... Norwich'.

8. As for instance with the identification of cloth-dying vats on Westwick Street: A. Carter and J.P. Roberts, 'Excavations in Norwich - 1972. The Norwich Survey - Second Interim Report', Norfolk Archaeology XXXV, 1973, pp.461, fig.6, and 464-7.

9. There is a gap of thirty-seven years between 1340 and 1377 and a second short gap of eight years after 1399, W. Hudson and J.C. Tingey Revised Catalogue of the Records of the City of Norwich (Norwich n.d) p.14; thereafter the number of enrolments per year drops from the 13th/14th-century average of *c*. 80 to less than 20.

10. The Norfolk Record Office also has details of where the duplicate copies of this archive are housed.

11. Legal jurisdiction within the walls of medieval Norwich was divided among a number of institutions (a concise account of their territories is given in Campbell, Norwich, Appendix III p.24). The enrolled deeds with which this booklet is concerned were the property of the City Court and relate, therefore, only to the area of its jurisdiction.

12. See pp.13 and 64.

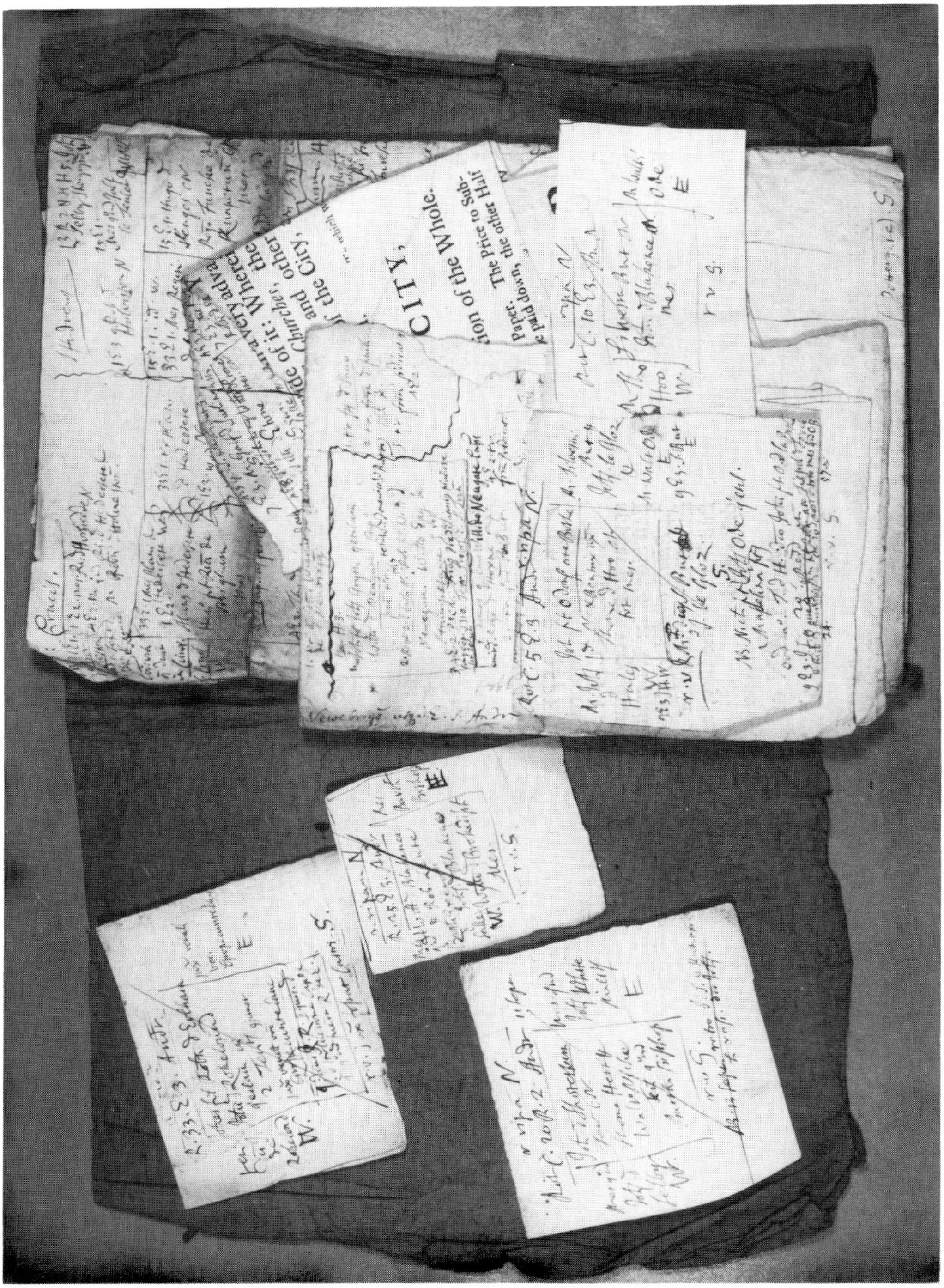

Pl.1

John Kirkpatrick's deed extracts for St Andrew's parish

THE ACQUISITION BY THE NORWICH BLACKFRIARS OF THE SITE FOR THEIR CHURCH *c.*1310—1325

by

Margot Tillyard

One aim of Helen Sutermeister's analysis of the Norwich enrolled deeds was the reconstruction of the city's topography and its pattern of property ownership in the period around 1300 AD. To do this the evidence of the deeds[1] had to be abstracted and plotted by hand onto a series of large coloured plans which are now deposited in the Norfolk Record Office. By taking one sheet of these plans as an example it is hoped to provide an introduction to their compilation, and an indication of the uses to which they may be put. The plan chosen (see fold-out at end of volume) shows the southern half of the site acquired by the Dominican or Black Friars for building their new monastery, and covers an area bounded by St George's Street on the west, Elm Hill on the east, and St Andrew's Street on the south; northwards the monastery extended as far as the river.

The site's long connection with the Friars, and the fact that the site was transferred to the city authorities at the Reformation, mean that it is particularly well documented throughout its history.[2] The majority of the property deeds used in the reconstructions were those enrolled in the city court, together with some of the so-called Private Deeds[3] (the original documents passed between buyer and seller), and a few from among the records of the Dean and Chapter.[4] As both these last sometimes record transactions not enrolled with the main series, they provide valuable supplementary information. The large majority of the deeds in both series relate to the direct transfer of property from one person to another, but there were various other types of transactions, which are discussed fully in Elizabeth Rutledge's paper, and will not, therefore, need to be described here. What matters as far as the plan-making is concerned is that, whatever the nature of the exchange, the property itself is always located by parish, sometimes with the addition of a named street, and normally with a record of the names of owners of adjoining properties, or some other identification of its position. This enables a link to be established between adjacent tenements.

The information obtained from the court rolls and the Private Deeds was calendered onto index cards, with the abuttals (data from adjacent property) round the edge, the top of the card representing north, as shown in Fig. 1 (overleaf).

The resulting slips were then sorted, matching street orientation, buyers, sellers and abuttals, so that a diagram of site ownership could be constructed, giving the names of successive holders of the properties over the period covered by the deeds. On the Blackfriars plan the abuttal data have been omitted for the sake of clarity, except where, as in the case of the lane and the small property in the south-west corner, they are the only source of information. On the plans for the whole of the city this data is written along the appropriate property boundaries, and can be expected to correspond to the names found in the main transactions.

Reference	Date	Parish
	Northern abuttal	
	Seller to Buyer	
	Subject of transaction Other details if any	
	Southern abuttal	

Fig.1 Form of deed abstract (cf. Pl.1).

The first person to realise the potential of this kind of reconstruction was the Norwich antiquarian John Kirkpatrick in the first quarter of the 18th century, and his notes clearly indicate that he attempted a similar exercise to ours (Pl.1).[5] His manuscript, published in 1889 as Streets and Lanes of the City of Norwich,[6] is perhaps the greatest source of help when studying the medieval city, as it lists all the streets and gives much additional information not available elsewhere. The earliest informative map of Norwich was that of Thomas Cleer, published in 1696,[7] which was used by Kirkpatrick. An excellent plan by Anthony Hochstetter appeared in 1789,[8] and, in addition, the 1885 Ordnance Survey proves useful for its extreme accuracy, and for the clarity with which both parish and individual property boundaries are shown. Also of great value are the large-scale maps incorporating medieval features included in James Campbell's work.[9] All these sources were helpful in attempting to integrate medieval property ownership with the city topography; but, in fact, because the pattern of the main streets has changed so little, it is relatively easy even today to relate the medieval plan to the modern one.

Up to 1307 the Blackfriars had occupied a large but non-riparian site in the parish of St Clement, north of the River Wensum, in the ward of the city known as 'Over the Water'. In that year they acquired the land and the buildings of the defunct Penitential or Sack Friars. The new site was nearer the city centre, and gave them access to the river, but there was no church worthy of their numbers or large enough for the congregations they hoped to attract. So, with the permission of the king, they set about purchasing the land between the old Penitential Friars' property and Wymer Street (the present St Andrew's Street) the main east to west thoroughfare of the city.[10] It can be seen from the reconstruction (Fig.2, fold-out at end) that, with one exception, the last transaction recorded for each property is its acquisition by the Blackfriars (or Friars Preachers as they are described in the deeds). Also, sometime between 1314 and 1319, as appears from information obtained from transactions concerning the property on the north-east corner of the reconstruction, they acquired the lane which dog-legs across the site, running in front of the Penitential Friars' buildings, then turning south to join Wymer Street a little to the east of its junction with the present St George's Street. Almost immediately after consolidating their ownership of the whole block, they set about building a fitting church, aligning it east to west and using every available foot of length.

The block of property acquired by the Friars between 1310 and 1325 comprised at least twelve messuages straddling three parishes; the boundaries of these parishes are marked on the map by dotted lines. It is satisfactory to be able to determine the limits of one, St Christopher's, which had disappeared by 1286. Other 'lost' parishes in the city emerged in the same way during the compilation of the plans: one example, further west along Wymer Street, was the parish of St Cross, which was divided between St Andrew and St John Maddermarket after the Reformation. The boundaries appear not to have been sacrosanct at this period; in a few cases a property described as being in one parish is assigned to another a few years later. Such uncertainties, where parishes interlock in areas with none too simple a street pattern, make for difficulties when drawing up reconstructions. As far as the Blackfriars are concerned, since their Order forbade them to own property apart from their monastic site,[11] it is a fair assumption that anything sold to them is likely to have been within this block. However, the ban may not have been strictly adhered to, as two exceptions have been noted: one example occurs in an indenture of 1276, by which the Master of the Hospital of St Giles leased to Henry de Senges a messuage identified only as situated in St Andrew's parish, at a rent of 6s per annum payable to the Friars Preachers, who were also licensed to distrain for the rent should it fall into arrears. (Henry was to be responsible for the repairs, and he was forbidden to dispose of the lease to religious persons or Jews.)[12] A second example is revealed by a post-Dissolution receipt dated 1540 sent by Henry VIII to Augustine Steward of Norwich. Steward, acting for the city, had paid £81 for property in St Clement's parish described as 'parcell of the possessions of the late Black Fryers'.[13]

The reconstruction provides useful evidence of the form of surname used at this date. The entries on the plan for the property next along the lane from the north-east corner begin: '1286. Executor of Agnes le Glover to Adam Beneyt de Suthrepps - transfer of messuage with buildings'.[14] These surnames are examples of two of the most common types - locative names indicating the origin of the holder's family, and names based on trade. It may be that glove-making was, in fact, practised on the site in question, as, from abuttal evidence, it appears that the subsequent holders of this property were Adam le Gaunt or le Gaunter (glover) - who may have been the same person as Adam Beneyt - and later Colyc the Glover. Norman-French and English forms seem to have been used indiscriminately at this period, and a Latin version is often found, possibly used only by scribes. People were frequently known by several names: the 'John, son of Adam de Stirston', clerk, who acquired the property next to Adam le Gaunter in 1292, is the same as the 'John del Stonhus', who held William But in fee on the west side of the lane. That he had two names may be inferred from abuttal information here, and proved by reference to reconstructions of other parts of the city.

This same property, which John, son of Adam de Stirston, acquired in 1292, was sold by John But to the Blackfriars in 1312, and this entry is interesting because it records a measurement of 'Forty feet by thirty feet'. Such rare additions to the almost universal description of properties simply as 'messuages with buildings' are valuable and were always entered on the reconstructions. On this reconstruction for instance, three more measurements are recorded - in addition to a cottage, half a well and a bakery with shops. Such details are what one might expect from a site near, but not in, the heart of the City. Further out towards the city walls, where average sizes of properties were larger, there are instances of arable land, dovehouses and barns; in commercially more valuable areas, average street frontages were often less than twenty feet, and groups of shops were common. Wells, or shares in wells, were quite often sold, as was the case when the property on the south-east corner of the printed reconstruction was divided in 1264. However, most people, no doubt, had to rely on a shared supply; although the only references to public wells or springs in the deeds under discussion are to 'St Lawrence's well', 'le Welleyard' in St Gregory's parish, and an unlocated one in St Andrew's.[15]

As is usual, no hint is given in the deeds of the materials used in the construction of the houses on the Blackfriars site. When the 'new room' of Adam le Rhymer on Holmestrete (now Bishopgate) is mentioned,[16] or the 'solar newly built' on the front of William de Sessons' house in Conesford Street (now King Street),[17] the deeds remain silent on this point. Only 'stone' (probably Northamptonshire limestone or flint) was deserving of mention, and such houses were clearly rare, as only ten are noted in the whole of the city.

The trades of property holders given on the Blackfriars plan present a typical range of those citizens with capital to spare - merchants, clerics of all types, provision merchants such as fishmen and bakers, and skilled tradesmen such as smiths, tailors and glaziers, most of whom had interests in other parts of the city also. Unrepresented on the plan, but common among Norwich property holders, were members of the clothworking and leatherworking groups such as dyers and tanners, institutions such as Holy Trinity Priory and St Giles Hospital, and occasional members of the gentry.[18] It was not until later that the city itself entered the property market in a drive to increase its income.

The name which appears more often on the printed reconstruction than any other is that of William But, a member of a prominent Norwich family. A William But was bailiff fourteen times between 1287 and 1317, and from 1327 his son William carried on the tradition, although he did not serve with such frequency. With the exception of a William But described as a hosier (that is, a leather gaiter maker), in a transaction in the tanners' market in 1291,[19] Buts are always described in the deeds as 'merchants', and they were involved in so many property transactions that one can only assume that they were the financiers of the period. (There are one hundred and ten entries under 'But' in Walter Rye's indexes to the deeds of 1285-1341.)[20] They dealt in large parcels of rents as well as in messuages. For instance, in 1303, William But acquired from Adam de Saham rents totalling £4 10s per annum in the parishes of St Cross, St Andrew, St Peter Mancroft, St Swithin and St John Berstrete.[21] These were all high-class rents from market stalls and from properties held by such prosperous tradesmen as goldsmiths and cordwainers in the centre of the city. The rent in St Andrew's parish was 5s per annum payable by Roger Godyng. It is tempting to link this rent with the easternmost St Andrew's property on the printed reconstruction, which Roger Godyng acquired in 1305, and which he made over to William But in 1325. It is common at this period to find a rent on a property passing to a new owner before the property itself.

William But made four properties over to the Blackfriars. West of the lane, in St Andrew's parish, were two properties he had been holding from John del Stonhus, and in 1308 he acquired John's interest in them both. Two years later he sold them to the Friars. In the same year William But acquired from Simon de Tacolneston his property to the south of the first two, which Simon had only owned for two years, and straightaway sold it to the Friars. The other properties he sold to them will be discussed later. Of the remaining two properties in this block, nothing is known of how the Friars acquired the one in the north-west corner, given in an abuttal as still belonging to the Priory of Holy Trinity in 1310, and though Kirkpatrick says that the Friars acquired the small piece on the south-west corner from Robert Fevere, from deed evidence, his name, in its form of Faber, is known only from the abuttals of the neighbouring properties.

The part of the site in the former parish of St Christopher consists of two large properties, running through from road to lane, and one smaller one. Thomas Chapman acquired the one to the east of the lane in 1297, and it remained in his hands until he sold it to the Friars in 1312. The former property of William Piket to the east was bought by Sylvester Sparwe in two parts in 1303 and 1305, and he kept it until he sold it to the Friars in 1311. The smaller property was acquired by William But in 1325 from Roger de Pulham, who had had it twenty years. Abuttal information indicates that he had already sold the next property to the east to the Friars by this time, and no doubt he followed suit with this one without delay (and it is assumed that the measurement of 'ninety-three feet by forty-four feet' given by Kirkpatrick refers to the two of them together).[22]

The fortunes of the remaining properties, which are all in St Peter Hungate, can be summarised briefly. The smaller ones in the north-east corner were all sold to the Friars between 1312 and 1314 by owners who had had them for a number of years. John But had owned his for at least nine years, Adam Blickling his for eleven, and Adam de Suthrepps, the father of Egidia, who sold hers to the Friars in 1313, had bought it twenty-seven years before.

The larger property at the south-east corner of the site had been split up before the Friars acquired it. The whole had been owned by a baker, and on his death in 1264, the eastern half, with the bakery and shops, was sold outside the family. John de Hengham acquired the northern half of this in 1310, and three years later disposed of it to the Friars. The western half remained in the family until the baker's grand-daughter's husband sold it to William But in 1315. It is not clear when he sold it to the Friars (as mentioned above). However, the eventual owner of the extreme south-east corner, Adam de Dalling, who acquired that in 1306, also had an interest in the property as a whole, which he made over to the Friars in 1322.

In conclusion, most of the property sold to the Friars had been in the hands of its owners for many years. The exceptions are those properties sold to William But. It is impossible to say whether he bought them as a speculation on his own account, or whether he was acting in some way as the Friars' agent. Either way he could not but gain. Unfortunately the deeds give no information about prices, except to make it clear that the Friars did indeed pay for the properties. For example, when William But (and his wife) handed over to them in 1310 the two pieces of land west of the lane (at the same time as another piece on the river with a quay), he did so *pro quadam sumam pecunie quam eis dederunt permanibus*.[23] However, as the process took at least fifteen years, perhaps the various owners held the Friars to a fair settlement.

In his book on the history of the Religious Orders in Norwich, Kirkpatrick quotes a Royal Charter of 1345 listing the Blackfriars' acquisitions after 1307.[24] When the reconstruction had been completed this list was compared with it. The names of the sellers corresponded, the four measurements given by the deeds were corroborated, and the remainder of the measurements given by Kirkpatrick enabled the map to be drawn roughly to scale. On the printed reconstruction the measurements from Kirkpatrick's list are overprinted in red.

In many ways this is a typical reconstruction: the type of information available, the sizes of the properties and the particulars of the owners are what might be expected from a site near the city centre. The additional information provided by Kirkpatrick's quoted list of dimensions strengthens the conviction that, while the precise shapes of the properties must remain conjectural, their relation to each other is correct. However, only the Friars at this period acquired such large blocks of holdings and obliterated property boundaries, so this is no ordinary site. We know what happened to the northern part of it because the church bears testimony; but what happened to the south? How large was the preaching yard? Where was the Great Gate of the Friary? Was it perhaps across the southern end of the lane which formerly crossed the site? When the Friars leased land to William Alman, haberdasher, in 1537,[25] so that he could build a house in the south-west corner of their precinct, did he re-occupy an earlier messuage? What is the history of the present buildings in the south-east corner of the site? The answers to these questions will have to await further documentary research.

ENDNOTES

1. Norfolk Record Office (hereafter NRO), Norwich City Records, case 1, shelf a, rolls 1-13. (Hereafter, references to the court rolls will give roll and membrane numbers only.)

2. For details about the Blackfriars in Norwich see J.Kirkpatrick, *History of the Religious Orders and Communities and of the Hospitals and Castle of Norwich* (London 1845); W.Hudson and J.C.Tingey (eds.), *The Records of the City of Norwich* I and II (Norwich 1906 and 1910); H.Sutermeister, *The Norwich Blackfriars* (Norwich 1977).

3. NRO, Norwich City Records, Private Deeds, cases 3 and 4 (hereafter PD).

4. NRO, Dean and Chapter Records, Norwich Deeds (hereafter DC).

5. NRO, case 21, shelf f.

6. J.Kirkpatrick, *Streets and Lanes of the City of Norwich*, written *c*. 1725, ed. W.Hudson (Norwich 1889).

7. Colman and Rye Library, Norwich, PS MN 4699.

8. Colman and Rye Library, Norwich, drawer C.

9. J.Campbell, *Norwich* (fascicle of the *Historic Town Plans Atlas*, London 1975).

10. Kirkpatrick, *Religious Orders ...* pp.24-28.

11. G.R.Galbraith, *Constitution of the Dominican Order* (Manchester 1925) p.36.

12. PD, St Andrew 1.8.

13. NRO, case 8, shelf k.

14. References to deeds written on the plan are not repeated in these notes; unless otherwise specified the references are to enrolled deeds. Private Deeds bear the prefix PD and Dean and Chapter deeds DC.

15. PD, St Lawrence 4; Roll 4, m.17d (unless so qualified references are to recto); and PD, St Andrew 1.8.

16. PD, Holmstrete 63, 66 and 67.

17. Roll 2, m.39d.

18. The trades and occupations of the property owners are discussed in Serena Kelly's paper.

19. Roll 2, m.37.

20. W.Rye, *A short calendar of deeds relating to Norwich enrolled in the court rolls of that city 1285-1306* (Norwich 1903), and *Calendar of Norwich deeds enrolled in the court rolls of that city 1307-1341* (Norwich 1915).

21. Roll 4, m.10.

22. Kirkpatrick, *Religious Orders ...*, p.26.

23. Roll 5, m.23.

24. Kirkpatrick, *Religious Orders ...*, p.26.

25. PD, St Andrew IV 21.

THE ECONOMIC TOPOGRAPHY AND STRUCTURE OF NORWICH *c*.1300

by

Serena Kelly

INTRODUCTION

The purpose of this paper is to give an impression of the economic structure of the City of Norwich during the late 13th and early 14th centuries by means of an analysis of all trades and occupations recorded in the deeds enrolled in the city court between 1285 and 1311.[1] The deeds survive virtually complete for this period, and, although they have certain limitations as a basis for quantitative conclusions, they provide a unique and valuable source for a study of the early economy of Norwich. There are few English cities where such comprehensive information is available for this period, for while some towns possess Freemen's Rolls from the 12th century, the data they provide before the 16th century is often scanty.[2]

The chief limitation in the use of the deeds for a study of the economy is the fact that, since the recording of a person's means of livelihood was incidental and not a legal requirement, by no means all the individuals named can be associated with a particular trade or occupation, and those who cannot be so linked are obviously excluded.[3] The number of parties involved in, or incidental to, property transactions recorded between the years 1285 and 1311 totals 3851. This figure (the 'deed population') comprises not only buyers and sellers, and their wives where appropriate, but also all those named as owners of abutting tenements, or as former owners of the property being transferred or of neighbouring properties. In other words, apart from court officials and witnesses, it covers all individuals recorded in the deeds in whatever context, each counted once only. Of this total, only 966, or 25%, have a trade assigned to them, and it is this figure which is referred to in the text as the 'known-trade population'. It represents only those whose occupation is specifically described; trade by-names (e.g. Thomas Lindraper) have been omitted from the count because of the uncertainty of knowing whether these were inherited or current.[4]

Apart from the obvious disadvantage, that the trades of the greater part of the population are unknown, other difficulties arise. One cannot, for instance, be certain that all the property transactions of this period were enrolled in the city court,[5] nor can the proportion of property owners to the total population be calculated.[6] It is likely, of course, that the buyers and sellers of property were among the wealthier citizens of Norwich, and are disproportionately represented in comparison with poorer tradesmen.[7] Still another area of uncertainty is that concerning domicile: for the evidence is of ownership of property and not necessarily residence. It is rarely possible to distinguish owner-occupied from investment properties, and the fact that some individuals held multiple tenements, perhaps in more than one parish, and that rents and rights as well as leases were

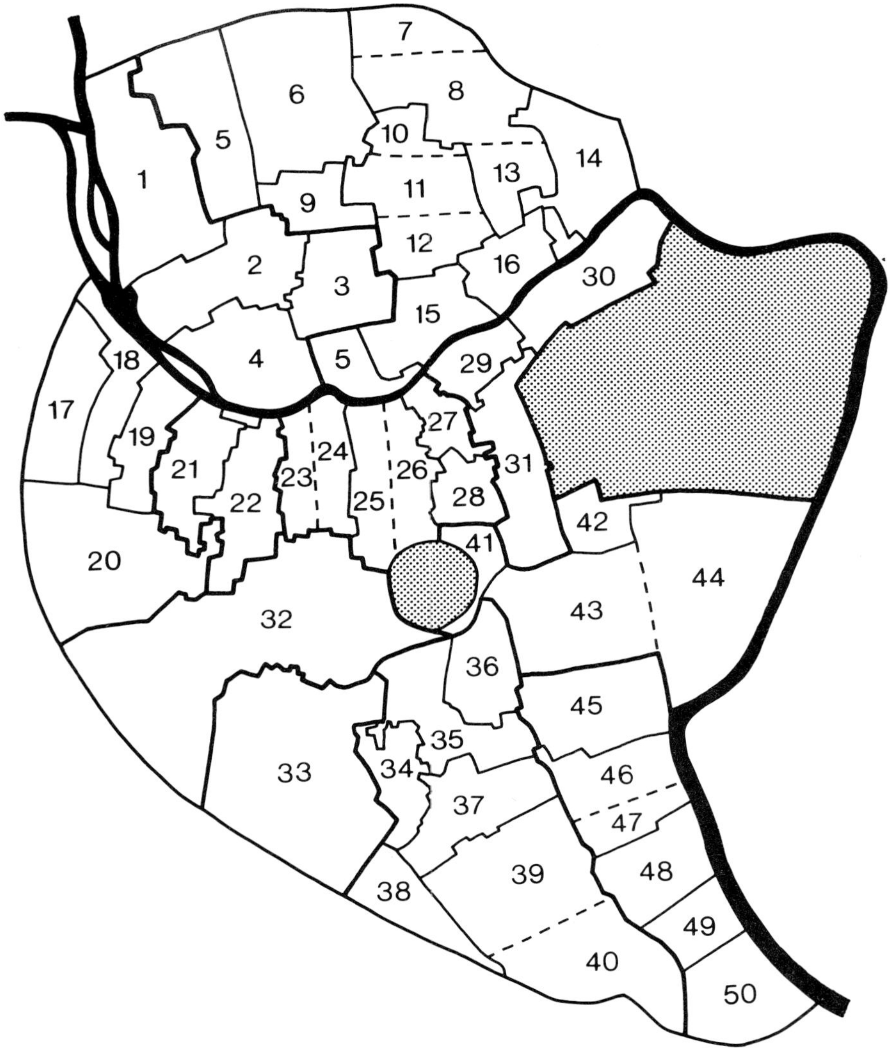

Fig.3

Norwich parishes c.1300, hypothetical boundaries being shown dashed. (The major areas outside city jurisdiction are shown stippled.)

ST MICHAEL COSLANY

1. St Martin Coslany
2. St Mary Coslany
3. St George Colgate
4. St Michael Coslany

ST GILES

17. St Benedict
18. St Swithin
19. St Margaret Westwick
20. St Giles

ST GREGORY

21. St Lawrence
22. St Gregory

ST ANDREW

23. St John Maddermarket
24. St Cross
25. St Andrew
26. St Christopher
27. St Peter Hungate
28. St Michael at Plea

ST GEORGE TOMBLAND

29. Sts Simon and Jude
30. St Martin at Palace
31. St George Tombland
32. St Peter Mancroft

ST CLEMENT FYEBRIDGE

5. St Clement Fyebridge (part
6. St Augustine -detached)
7. St Margaret Fyebridge
8. All Saints Fyebridge
9. St Olave
10. St Botolph
11. St Saviour
12. St Mary Combust
13. St Paul
14. St James
15. St Margaret Newbridge
16. St Edmund Fishergate

ST STEPHEN

33. St Stephen

BERSTRETE

34. All Saints Berstrete
35. St John Timberhill
36. St Martin Bailey
37. St Michael at Thorn
38. St Katherine
39. St Bartholomew
40. St John Sepulchre

NORTH CONESFORD

41. St Mary the Less
42. St Cuthbert
43. St Peter Parmountergate
44. St Vedast

SOUTH CONESFORD

45. St Michael Conesford
46. St Julian
47. St Clement Conesford
48. St Ethelreda
49. St Edward
50. St Peter Southgate

Fig.3

NORWICH PARISHES c.1300, GROUPED BY SUB-LEET

transferred, suggests a degree of speculation in real estate. The extent of that speculation, however, may have been relatively limited. Table 1 shows that, with only a few exceptions (such as the woolmen), the majority of individuals held property in only one parish.[8] Nevertheless, positive proof of residence, or place of business, which may not in any case have been the same will not be provided by the deed evidence alone.

When allowance is made for these limitations in the evidence it is seen that the deeds provide invaluable information on the sixty-eight separate services and trades recorded for Norwich between 1285 and 1311, for they enable an impressionistic picture of the relative importance of these trades and their geographical distribution to be drawn.[9]

To facilitate the processing of the voluminous and complex data contained in the enrolled deeds a computer was used; this had the advantage of allowing quick extraction of relevant data and of enabling checks to be made easily.[10] For the purposes of this paper the figures were consolidated in two ways. In the first place, the fifty medieval parishes for which deeds exist (Fig. 3) were grouped by sub-leet as shown in Fig. 4.[11] Secondly, the sixty-eight trades were divided into eleven categories (arranged here in order of numerical significance):

1. *Ecclesiastical*
2. *Leather*
3. *Textiles*
4. *Provisions*
5. *Merchant*
6. *Metal Trades*
7. *Clothing Trades*
8. *Building Trades*
9. *Miscellaneous*
10. *Service Trades*
11. *Agricultural*

These trade groups form the basis for the discussion which follows, and it is they and not individual trades that are mapped on Fig. 5. In the few cases where numbers in a trade fall below five, no attempt has been made in the text to draw conclusions from them, but the presence of the trade has, nonetheless, been recorded in the tables and illustrations.

The body of the paper considers each trade group in turn, beginning with the largest in terms of numbers. Broadly, each sub-division deals with the numbers involved in each trade followed by a consideration of their possible distribution throughout the city, with some speculation on the reasons for the siting of particular industries. Discussion in the text of the numbers and distribution of individuals in a particular trade is based on the known-trade population. As has been explained above, the deed population and the known-trade population figures were based on counting each individual once only. But since a number of the city's inhabitants had multiple property interests (Table 1), another method of assessment was needed to show the full extent and distribution of holdings by the members of each trade. To arrive at this, individuals were counted once in each sub-leet in which they were involved in property exchanges. The total of interests thus calculated was 1172 and it is this 'trades-interest' figure which is broken down, by sub-leet and by trade/trade group, in Tables 2 and 3.

The information is expressed graphically in two ways. On Fig. 5 a contrast is first drawn between the size of each sub-leet's deed population and the number of its trades-interests (these are expressed by means of circles, the areas of which vary in proportion to the numbers involved). The trades-interest figures are then sub-divided

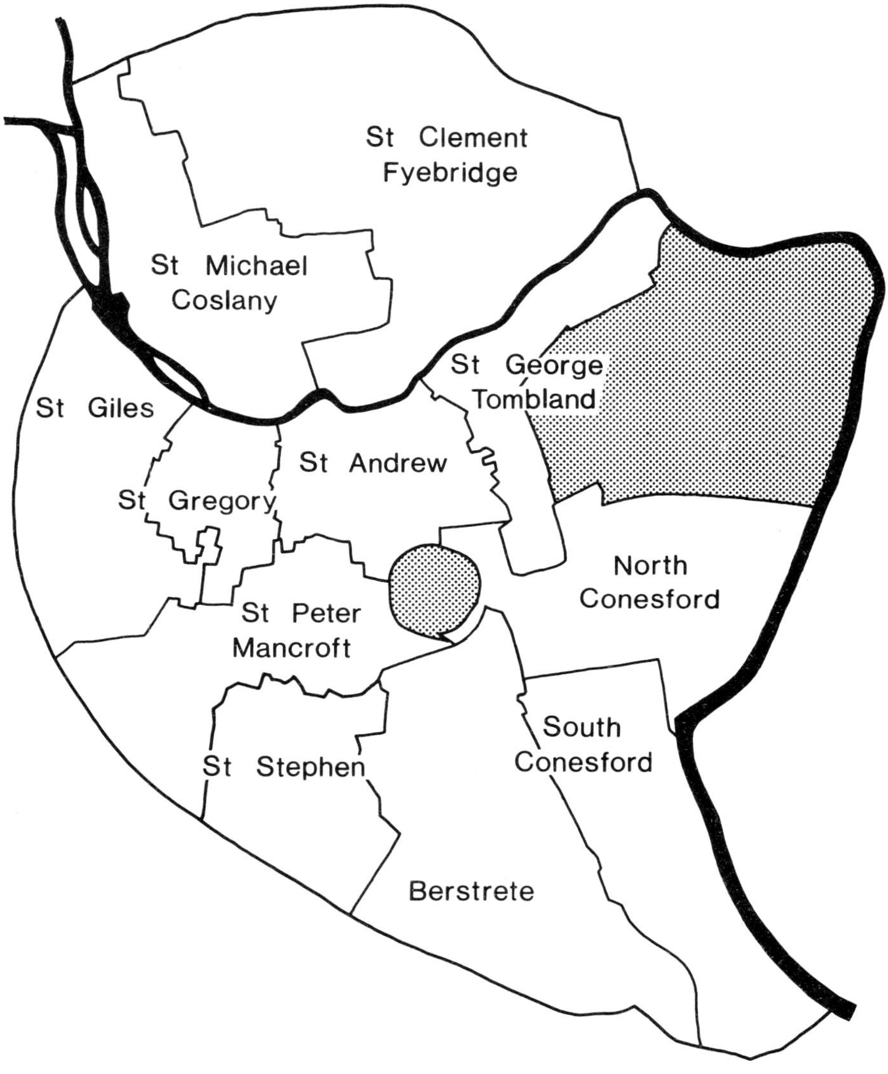

Fig.4

Norwich sub-leets c.1300

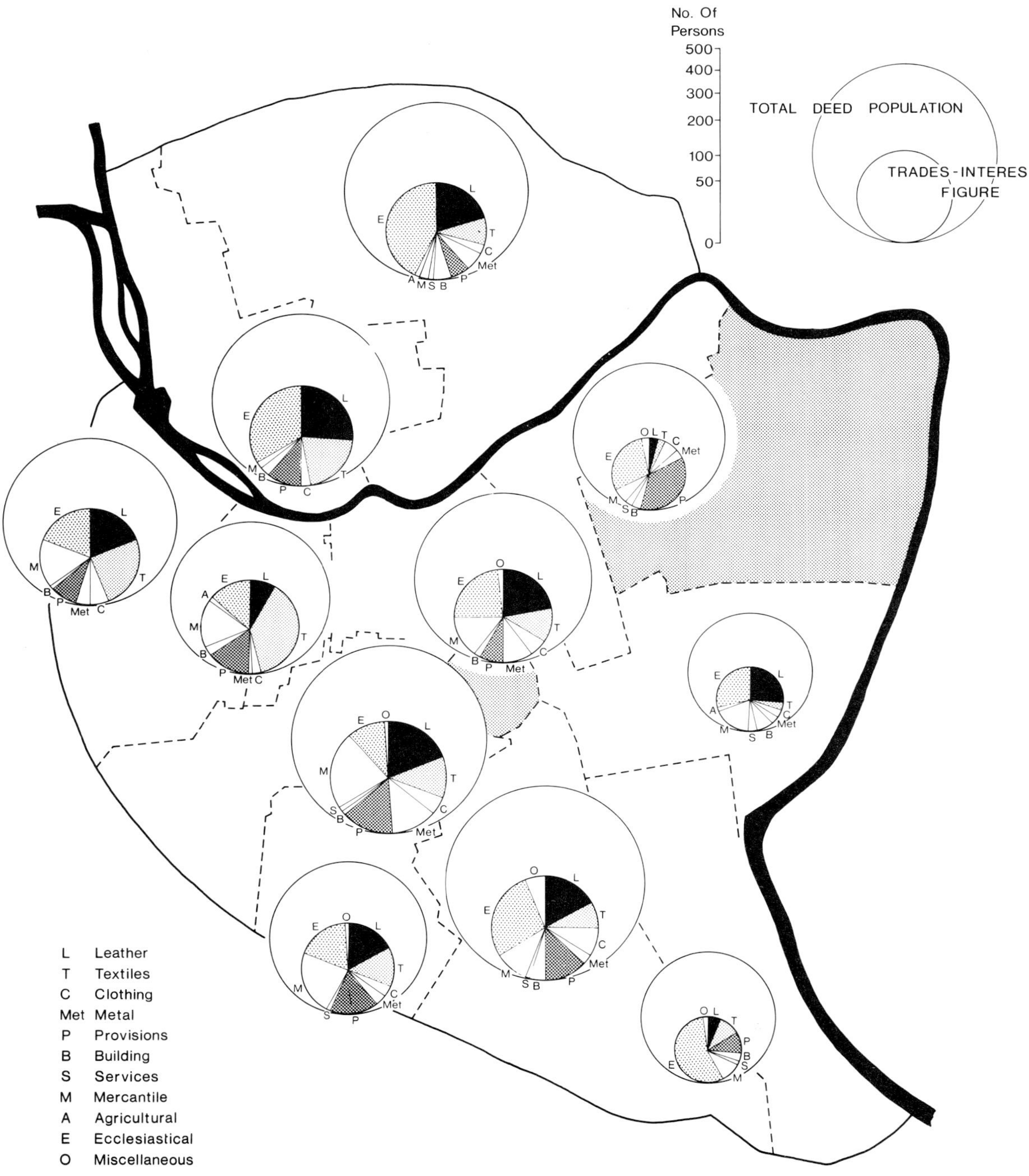

Diagrammatic map of the economic topography of Norwich c.1300. This shows: a) the proportional relationship between the deed population and the trades-interest figure (p.16) for each sub-leet; b) the trades-interest figures divided by trade groups. Cf. Table 3.

to show the percentage involved in each trade group. In contrast the histograms in Fig. 6 show the trades-interest figures as a percentage of the deed population for each sub-leet.

ANALYSIS BY TRADE GROUP

ECCLESIASTICAL

By far the largest occupational group recorded is that of the ecclesiastics, who together include 247 individuals, or 25% of the known-trade sample. Almost half of these (119) were chaplains while, clerks (some of whose ecclesiastical status is in doubt) were the next most numerous category. Smaller numbers of rectors, vicars and parsons are recorded as holding property and there are incidental references to three anchorites.

Chaplains were involved in property exchanges in every sub-leet of the city, with concentrations in the parishes of St Peter Mancroft and St Olave. A wide variety of property changed hands: as well as the more usual conveyances of messuages, land and rent, grants were made of 'an orchard with land and appurtenances', 'two shops under one roof', 'land with a kiln' (*torallo*), and in St Augustine's parish in 1292, John de Birston, chaplain, was granted a piece of land *cum orrea* (with a barn).[12] Such a diversity of interests could possibly be explained by the fact that the chaplains were acting as trustees in property transactions, and the reconstructions were checked to see if this could be confirmed. The results, however, were inconclusive: the majority of the eighty-seven properties looked at gave no further information about the chaplain, and in a further twenty-five cases it could be seen that he remained in continuous possession for anything up to twenty years. It would seem more likely, therefore, that the commercial and agricultural properties in which they were dealing were bought for personal investment and as a source of rent income.[13]

Clerks represent the second most numerous group within the ecclesiastical category: sixty-nine individuals (approximately 7% of the known-trade population) being so described. It is doubtful however, whether all were in holy orders, for seven of them were identified by Blomefield as officials of the city, either as bailiffs, town clerks or *custodes* (keepers).[14] Whether these were married, and therefore probably not priests,[15] is unknown, but thirty-three others, perhaps scrivenors, were certainly associated with their wives in property transactions. As no differentiation was made in the deeds between these groups of clerks, they have all been included with the ecclesiastics. North of the river there were concentrations of clerks involved with property in the sub-leets of St Clement (sixteen) and St Michael Coslany (twelve). They were also well represented in all the sub-leets to the south, although the numbers were not as high. Only in North Conesford sub-leet, where two clerks are recorded, does the figure fall dramatically below the average; there is no obvious reason for this. The fact that some were engaged in property grants of shops, stalls and selds in the market area of St Peter Mancroft parish, and in empty land in the Gildencroft or suburbs of the city supports Heath's contention that 'for the most part such clerks who were of age lived as laymen and worked their patrimony or found other secular employment'.[16] It is, however, at least as likely that they were investing their financial resources in such properties and regarding them as sources of rent income. As with the chaplains, a check of the reconstructions does not provide any evidence that the clerks were acting as trustees: for in 45% of cases either the clerk

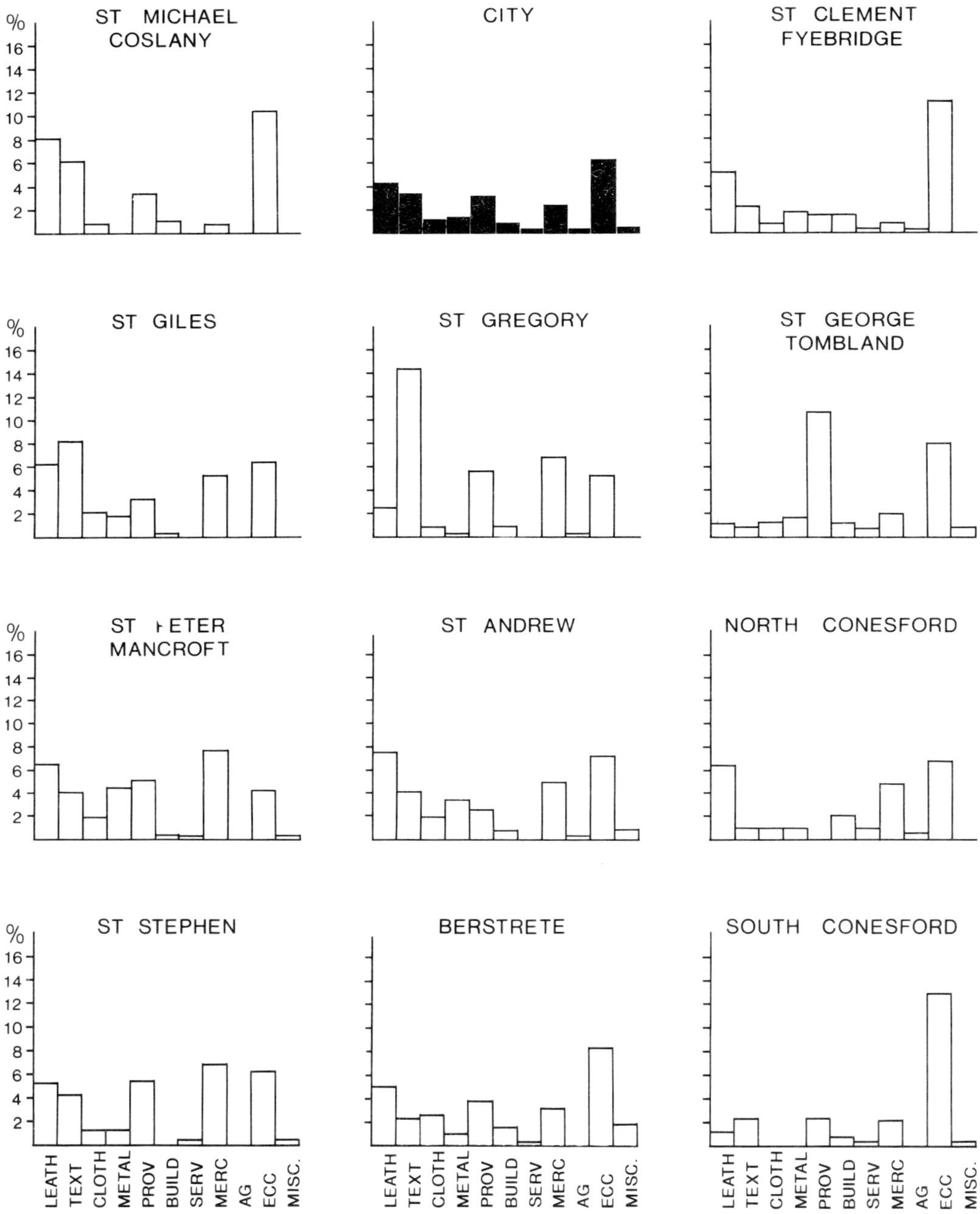

Fig.6

Trades-interest figures shown as a percentage of the deed populations of the sub-leets and of the city as a whole

or his wife were still holding the property up to forty-three years later, and in 54% of the cases no further information regarding the clerk is recorded.

Other members of the ecclesiastical heirarchy represented in the deeds are rectors (thirty-seven individuals, or nearly 4% of the known-trade population), parsons (fifteen), vicars (four) and anchorites (three). Except for the anchorites, they are recorded in every sub-leet of the city, but in common with other ecclesiastics, they seemed to favour the two sub-leets north of the river. In nearly 70% of cases the names of the rectors, parsons and vicars are followed by the name of the parish of which they were the incumbent, but it is not clear whether they lived where their interests were, and held their benefices as absentees, or whether they used the properties merely for investment. Eight rectors were associated with specific Norwich churches, of which four held property interests in the same parish. The interests of a further two were not located in a particular parish, and two were involved with property in a different city parish. Roger, son of Henry the Goldsmith, for example, was the rector of St Botolph's, but in 1286 it is land in the parish of St Michael at Plea that he is recorded as selling.[17] Fifteen other property-holding rectors are recorded as holding livings in rural Norfolk (some as far away as Field Dalling and Bawsey[18]), but only one in Suffolk (Ilketshall St Mary[19]).

Of the fifteen men described as parsons, four were associated with Norwich churches (but one of them occurring in a parish not that of the church with which he was connected[20]) and seven held livings in Norfolk. Among the vicars was another Suffolk ecclesiastic, Philip de Wangford, of Reydon-next-the-Sea (near Southwold[21]) while the other three vicars mentioned in the deeds were attached to the parishes of Little Yarmouth, Hanworth and Narford.

Reference is made in the abuttals of certain deeds to three anchorites: Cecily, the anchorite of St Mary Combust;[22] Katerina, the anchorite of St Margaret, Newbridge;[23] and Alice de Thorpe,[24] the anchorite of All Saints, Swinemarket.

Representatives of religious institutions, such as the Cathedral Priory and the friaries, were also active in the land market at this time. As far as the Cathedral was concerned, in most instances references were made either to 'the Priory', or 'the Prior and Chapter', but other officials such as the cantor, the infirmarer and the almoner were also specified. These men were involved in property deals in the parishes of St Olave and St Augustine, north of the river, and St Andrews, St Giles and St Peter Parmountergate in the southern half of the city.

Of the four principal orders of friars known to have been present in Norwich at this time,[25] the Dominicans, the Franciscans and the Austin Friars were all involved in acquiring land for their sites.[26] Those most active were the Dominicans, as it was during the early part of the 14th century that they were in the process of moving from the site of their original foundation north of the river. Deeds therefore record both their original holding in St Clement Fyebridge and their acquisition, in 1310, of a valuable site in St Andrews with access to the river and a quay (see pp.5-10).

Other Norwich religious bodies involved with property at this time were the Chapel of St Mary in the Fields, Norman's Hospital, the

Great Hospital, Hildebrand's Hospital and the Magdalen Hospital. Seventeen religious bodies established in the county of Norfolk are represented in the deeds during this period, as are five from Suffolk. From further afield the Augustinian Canons from Waltham in Essex owned a house in St Edmund Fishergate,[27] and the Cistercian foundations of Woburn in Bedfordshire[20] and Garendon in Leicestershire[29] bought land along the riverside in St Peter Parmountergate. The only foreign ecclesiastical institution specified in the deeds is the Hospital of St Mary in Roncevaux, whose newly-appointed general proctor,[30] Brother Lupus, was recorded in 1293 selling land and rents in the parish of St Cross.[31]

The holdings of these ecclesiastical institutions were concentrated in the east and south of the city; and particularly marked is the incidence of ownership of quays and other riverside properties. In some cases, as with the friars, these were acquired as part of their precincts and need have had no commercial significance.[32] These and the other ecclesiastically-owned private quays upstream of Bishop's Bridge (those of the Great Hospital, the Leper Hospital of St Mary Magdalen and the Prior[33]) might have catered for 'passengers or for loads which were small, local or casual or which for some other reason did not incur customs'.[34] Downstream of Bishop's Bridge, where the major quays were probably located from the twelfth century onwards,[35] there is no evidence of the city exercising a wharfage monopoly before 1379,[36] although this might be suggested by the licensing in 1291 of the Archdeacon of Norfolk, Alan de Freston, to hold a quay. His interests, as of the Cistercians of Woburn and Garendon, and the Abbot of Wendling,[37] all recorded pre-1307, may well have been in the export of wool in what has been termed, as far as taxation is concerned, the 'pre-institutional stage' of the trade.[38]

LEATHER

The most substantial industrial grouping in Norwich c. 1300 was that of the leather workers. There are references to fifty-nine shoe-makers, fifty tanners, thirty-four skinners, seventeen tawyers, eight saddlers, three parchment makers and two whitawyers: a total of 173 men, forming 18% of the known-trade population. Members of this category were found in every sub-leet in the city, but were present in greatest numbers in the western and central areas: in particular along the river frontage in the sub-leets of St Michael Coslany, St Andrew and St Giles; in the market parish of St Peter Mancroft; and in the south of the city in Berstrete sub-leet. The Great Cockey, which ran north through St Stephen's, St Peter Mancroft and St Andrew's to the river,[39] no doubt provided water for the tanners, skinners and tawyers who held property interests in these parishes. The small number of leather workers in St George Tombland sub-leet may largely be explained by the fact that Fyebridge Quay occupied the available river frontage; on the opposite bank, in the sub-leet of St Clement Fyebridge, the trades were certainly present. Two small groups of tanners and skinners held property at either end of Conesford: one group in the parishes of St Peter Parmountergate and St Vedast (in the north of North Conesford), where they were presumably exploiting Barkeres (i.e. tanners') Fleet and other small streams which led to the river;[40] and the other group in St Peter Southgate parish at the southern end of South Conesford sub-leet. In between these groups King Street had been settled and developed by religious houses and wealthy or aristocratic families, whose own exploitation of the river frontage limited industrial expansion by other groups.

The largest sub-category within the leather trade grouping is that of the fifty-nine individuals engaged in the shoe trade, which comprises all those described variously as 'shoemakers', 'cordwainers', 'cobblers', and sutors. They were found throughout the city, apart from the sub-leets of North and South Conesford, but were prominent in the sub-leets of St Andrew and St Peter Mancroft, no doubt because of the proximity of the main city market. East of this, the street now known as Gentleman's Walk was called 'Cordwainers Row' in the 14th century,[41] but it is clear from the reconstructed tenement pattern of this area that no late-13th or early-14th-century shoemaker was buying or selling property along the street although they may well have been in occupation as tenants.[42] The sub-leets of St Giles and St Gregory were also close to the market, but the deed population of these sub-leets is heavily biased towards textile production, and it was only downstream in St Andrew's sub-leet that the numbers engaged in the leather trades exceeded those of the textile workers. Many of the shoemakers who held property in other parts of the city had additional interests in shops or stalls in the market, suggesting that they were bringing the manufactured goods into the market to sell as well as retailing from their workshops. Apart from the market transactions, messuages and rents form the bulk of the transfers by shoemakers.

The fifty tanners form the next largest sub-category within the leather trade grouping. They were present in every sub-leet in the city, but more than half (twenty-seven) were involved in transactions in the sub-leets of St Michael Coslany and St Clement Fyebridge. There, no doubt, they took advantage of the river frontage and the water supply from the streams flowing through these two sub-leets: the Water of Muspol; the Dalymond Dike; and a third watercourse which according to Kirkpatrick 'lies ... at the back of the Houses of the N. side of Fishergate and which also turns N. towards St Paul's church'.[43] The importance of access to water for the tanners is emphasised by the stipulation in several of the deeds that the property transferred (in most cases, messuages with land and buildings) included 'rights to watercourse'. Despite the fact that tanners have been described as 'notorious offenders in matters of public hygiene',[44] deed evidence alone does not suggest that public distaste consigned the Norwich tanners to specified areas of the city or that they were encouraged to pursue their trade outside the city walls.

The thirty-four skinners (who dealt in fine skins and furs) follow the tanners in numerical importance in this grouping. They were concerned with property in every sub-leet in the city with the exception of St George Tombland, but were present in the greatest numbers in Berstrete sub-leet. Surprisingly few skinners occurred in North Conesford where the street name 'Permountergate' would have suggested a concentration.[45] Skinners were involved in a small proportion of the transactions involving stalls or shops on Skinners' Row in the market area of St Peter Mancroft parish, but the majority of the property transfers among this occupational group concerned messuages with buildings and appurtenances elsewhere.

Tawyers, who 'dressed the skinners' pelts'[46] were also recorded in the deeds for this period. Seventeen of them held interests along the Westwick river frontage and in the sub-leets of St Peter Mancroft and St Stephen; clearly, the 'unsweete and unwholesome ayre'[47] associated with the process had not yet proved so significant as to cause the craft to be banned from the central areas of the city. Some tawyers during this period possessed shops and stalls in St Peter Mancroft parish and in the market, suggesting that they were involved in retailing manufactured articles as well as in the industrial processing of the raw material.

The location of the eight individuals recorded as saddlers, (concentrated in the sub-leets of Berstrete and St Peter Mancroft), seems not to have been tied to that of any other branch of the industry. Perhaps more important was the need to be where prospective customers could see, and order, what may have been custom-made items.

TEXTILES

From deed evidence alone, it would appear that the textile industry had not, in the early 14th century, assumed the pre-eminent position in the economy of Norwich that it was to enjoy from the 16th century onwards.[48] The numbers involved in it, though, (144 or 15% of the known-trade population) fall not far short of those in the leather trades (172). Thirty-four drapers form the largest of the ten sub-categories within the group; dyers are next most numerous (thirty); and twenty-seven linendrapers, fourteen weavers, twelve wool merchants, ten fullers, eight shearmen, six woad merchants, two quilterers and one flaxman follow. Although members of the trade group were present in every sub-leet, the majority are known from the western and central areas of the city. South of the river, the greatest concentrations were in the sub-leets of St Giles and St Gregory. Here, exceptionally, the leatherworkers were outnumbered, whereas downstream in St Andrew's sub-leet the normal pattern prevailed. Yet further downstream, as has already been noted for the leather trades, the river frontage may have been less available for industrial exploitation.

Individuals described without qualification as drapers (and therefore perhaps dealing in woollen textiles) were prominent in St Giles and St Peter Mancroft. The majority of transactions in St Peter Mancroft involved stalls and selds, which were probably used to retail cloth worked up elsewhere. The incidence of people described specifically as linendrapers was similar to that of the drapers, in that they were most numerous in the sub-leets of St Giles, St Peter Mancroft and St Stephen. They were absent from the eastern and southern parts of the city, and only three linendrapers held any property north of the river. The by-names of linendrapers such as Geoffrey de Salle, William de Cawston, Richard de Felmingham, Augustin de Aylsham and John de Blickling, all derived from names of villages in the same limited area, perhaps indicate a centre of the linen industry in the county north of Norwich.

The most striking concentration of any occupational group within a particular area of the city was that of the dyers in the sub-leet of St Gregory, where two-thirds of those mentioned in the deeds held property. This concentration was reflected in the name of one of the waterfront streets, known by 1307 as Letestere (Dyers') Row,[49] while a late medieval dye-house was discovered nearby in excavations undertaken by the Norwich Survey.[50] Dyers were also present in the sub-leet of St Giles to the west of St Gregory, and in St Michael Coslany to the north, thus forming a compact group in the western area of the city, with only isolated examples in other localities. The value attached to a riverside site is demonstrated by the exceptionally high price of twenty-five marks paid by a dyer, Adam Berd, for such a property in St Margaret Westwick.[51]

Only 10% of those involved in the textile trade belonged to the sub-category of weaver, for which the overall term <u>textor</u> was used in the deeds. This usage is in marked contrast to the variety of expressions[52] used by 1453 in what was then presumably a more specialised industry. In the 13th and early 14th centuries they were to be found mainly in the sub-leet of St Andrew, and were absent from the southern and eastern areas of the city. The small number of weavers indicated in the deeds, compared, for example to those engaged in dyeing or fulling, might indicate that, around 1300, Norwich was a finishing centre for cloth woven elsewhere in the county, although their absence from the deeds could suggest that they were too poor to own their own tenements. Nevertheless, one of their number, Robert de Holveston, achieved the important rank of bailiff in 1311.[53]

The ten individuals described as fullers in the deeds were all found in the western area of the city, which gave them access to relatively clean water, and also to open ground where their tenters could stand. Tentergrounds, where cloth was stretched on frames (tenters) after fulling, are mentioned only in St Giles parish and in Chapelfield.[54] Both deed and street-name evidence of the early to mid-14th century suggest that the fulling was then concentrated in the parishes of St Gregory and St John Maddermarket.[55] This would have been non-mechanised, but by 1429 there had been a shift to water-powered operation at the New Mills.[56] After the cloth was fulled and stretched on tenters the nap was trimmed by a shearman. Eight are recorded in the city deeds, mainly in the vicinity of Charing (or Shearing) Cross[57] in the sub-leet of St Gregory. Six woad merchants or 'weyders' are recorded in the north and west of the city, where the presence of other dye-merchants is suggested by the name of Maddermarket.[58]

It would seem that, by the early 14th century, the textile industry was already well established in Norwich, with a wide variety of occupations within the trade grouping. Individuals concerned with the various stages of cloth production were principally centred on the riverside sub-leets in the western area of the city in Westwick and Coslany. There were probably good reasons for this: the banks of the cockeys running down to the river in North Conesford were taken up by leather workers; the waterside in the great bend of the river was either hopelessly marshy or controlled by the Cathedral; while the river in South Conesford was not only lined with staithes and warehouses, but would also have been polluted by effluent from the whole city.

PROVISIONS

The provisions trades are represented in the deed sample by forty-three bakers, thirty-eight fishers, seventeen butchers, thirteen tavernkeepers seven cooks, five poulterers, five spicers and two apothecaries. Together they form 14% of the known-trade population. These tradesmen were found in every sub-leet of the city, with the exception of North Conesford, but were far more numerous south of the river, and were heavily biased towards the market area of St Peter Mancroft and the area outside the Cathedral gates in the parish of St George Tombland. The relative scarcity of individuals engaged in provisioning north of the river possibly reflects a lower density of population.

The forty-three bakers recorded in the deeds were found scattered throughout the city, although their numbers are fewer in the north and very south. This wide distribution may suggest that they were not necessarily relying on the main market of St Peter Mancroft to sell their produce, although it is possible that bread was carried to the market to be sold from baskets. Three bakeries and two half shares in bakeries were referred to in the sub-leets of St Andrew, St Gregory, St Michael Coslany and St Stephen. Only on two occasions were stalls specifically described as being in the market area.

Fishers were not, as might be expected, active all along the river frontages of the city. The deeds do reveal their presence along the river in Westwick and in the sub-leets of St George Tombland, St Andrew and St Clement Fyebridge, but with two exceptions they were absent from the river frontage in Conesford. The largest concentration occurred in St George Tombland, where the retail outlets of the area outside the Cathedral gates may have been more important than proximity to the riverside as a locational factor. They also held interests in St Peter Mancroft parish, where they had stalls on Fishmongers' Row. One fish-house (fischusum) is recorded in St George Tombland parish and shops are mentioned also in the parishes of St Mary and St Michael Coslany. There are references in the Leet Rolls to the organisation of the retailing of fish, but the example of Ranulph the fishmonger, who was amerced 84 times in 1288 for 'forstalment and forbarment of fish', suggests that enforcement of the regulations was not thorough going.[59]

The seventeen butchers present in the deed sample were confined to the sub-leets of Berstrete, St Peter Mancroft, St Stephen and St Andrew, with the largest number (nine) occupying land in Berstrete. One reason for this localisation would undoubtedly have been to limit the offensive effects of their trade to a specific area, but an important reason could also be that Ber Street lies between the point of entry of cattle into the city at Carrow and their point of sale in the market. That cattle were fattened on the marshes immediately outside the city is suggested by the surnames of two butchers, John Gerard of Trows and Roger Fleghe of Trows, and with others they could have exploited the grazing on St Katherine's Plain and the Butter Hills.[60] The dedication of the church halfway down Ber Street to St Bartholomew (who is closely connected with the butchering trade)[61] suggests that this concentration of butchers was not a medieval development but a continuation from an earlier period.[62]

The thirteen tavernkeepers recorded in the deeds for this period were found in the sub-leets of St Stephen, St Andrew, St Clement Fyebridge and St Gregory, with two marked concentrations in the parishes of St Peter Mancroft and St George Tombland. The former concentration must be associated with the main city market; while the attraction of Tombland may well have been not just its weekly market and fairs[63] but, much more importantly, its proximity to the centres of ecclesiastical and county administration at the Cathedral and Castle, and to the legal centre of St Michael at Plea.[64] Tavernkeepers were involved mainly in transfers of messuages and land, although both John de Walsham and John de Elmeswelle had interests in shops in St George Tombland and St Peter Mancroft respectively. John de Elmeswelle, then described as 'innkeeper' also made substantial acquisitions in 'Overowe', a street in St Peter Mancroft. There, in 1302, he became the owner of one messuage with buildings, and one with a cellar and 'solar' (a rarity at this date).[65]

Cooks would have been attracted to St George Tombland for the same reasons as the tavernkeepers, and their presence is recorded in the street name 'Cockrowe' from 1314 onwards.[66] Only seven of these perhaps under-recorded tradesmen are known, and of these three were concerned with land in St Clement Fyebridge, and St Andrew. Again, two of the five poulterers mentioned in the deeds held interests in St George Tombland, while the other three were involved in the sub-leets of St Peter Mancroft, Berstrete and South Conesford. Five spicers and two apothecaries transferred property in Norwich at this date. Four of the former held interests in Berstrete, while the fifth was present in St Stephen.

In conclusion it would seem that there was a close connection between the provisioning trades and the sub-leet of St George Tombland, as this was where the majority of tavernkeepers, cooks, fishers and poulterers held property interests. It would seem that Tombland, as a provisioning centre, was one of the dispersed specialised markets (such as, for example, those for horses, pigs and cheese[67]) which operated away from the general market in St Peter Mancroft. It seems possible that its custom derived from a non-resident population, for it is these transients rather than the citizens who would have had most need of its services.

MERCHANTS

The term 'merchant' or, in one case, its variant 'mercer' was used as a description of ninety-seven different individuals in the deeds, who together form 10% of the known-trade population. The river formed a very clear boundary between those properties in which the merchants were interested and those in which they were not. To its north, the sub-leets of St Michael Coslany and St Clement Fyebridge were apparently considered not worth exploiting, as only five merchants were involved in property transactions there. South of the river, there was also a division between the western and eastern parts of the city in terms of areas attractive to mercantile interests. In the eastern sub-leets of St George Tombland, North and South Conesford, and to a lesser extent, Berstrete, merchants did not form a high percentage of those involved in property transactions, whereas they were clearly attracted to the western parts of the city. Not surprisingly, the largest concentration (thirty-four) was found in the market parish of St Peter Mancroft, and there were also large bodies of merchant interest in St Giles (twenty), St Gregory (twenty), St Stephen (twenty) and St Andrew (twenty). Interestingly, this distribution and intensity mirrors that of the later medieval brick-vaulted undercrofts found in the city.[68] The deeds do not reveal the commodities with which the merchants were involved, nor whether they exploited industrial properties themselves, or used them for investment purposes, but the descriptions of the properties they exchanged do indicate the diverse nature of their interests. Apart from the more usual instances of exchanges of houses, rents, messuages and land, merchants transferred tentergrounds and tenterframes in St Giles and Chapelfield, a bakery and a half share in a bakery in St John Maddermarket and St Gregory, a barn in St Stephen, 'a watermill at Westwyk fishery', and a fishhouse, as well as large numbers of shops and stalls. It would seem, therefore, that real wealth in the medieval urban community was accumulated by those of wide-ranging rather than specialised trading interests; while the large number of merchants in the medieval city who were obviously eager to exploit its advantages reinforces the impression of early-14th-century Norwich as a busy commercial centre providing a marketing function for a wide hinterland.[69]

METAL TRADES

The metal trades are represented in the deed sample by nineteen goldsmiths, sixteen smiths, eight cutlers, five lorimers, five latoners, two nedlerers, two furbishers, two bell-founders and one armourer. Together, they represent 6% of the known-trade population. In general, the trades tended to be centred on the sub-leets of St Peter Mancroft and St Andrew, with a significant concentration of smiths in the sub-leet of St Clement Fyebridge.

Nineteen goldsmiths, members of what Urry called 'the most

distinguished among the crafts',[70] were recorded in the Norwich deeds for this period. They were concentrated in the market parish of St Peter Mancroft, where their transfers (including 'four shops under one roof', 'three shops under one roof' and selds with yards) suggest that, in contrast to the smiths, who were absent from the market area, they were bringing finished articles into the market to sell. No goldsmith was active in the property market to the north of the river, which seems to have been both less prosperous and less populous than the rest of the city at this time.

The concentration of smiths in the sub-leet of St Clement Fyebridge may be linked with a tradition of iron-working to the north of the river. Archaeological evidence shows that, in the 12th and early 13th centuries, iron was being smelted from nodules dug from the gravel, while by c. 1300 the emphasis seems to have shifted to the smithing of, presumably, imported raw material.[71] Smithing in the city was located for the most part in the peripheral parishes, as would be expected from its anti-social character: not just its noise and smell,[72] but also the very considerable risk of fire. Their products, too, were perhaps most in demand by those travelling with horses, and by agricultural workers outside the walls. Whatever the reason, King's Lynn provides a parallel example of smiths situated on the boundaries of settlement.[73]

The existence of a street in St Peter Mancroft parish called Cutlers' Row[74] suggests that there was once a concentration of this trade there, but by c. 1300 this had dispersed, and furbishers and a fletcher, as well as cutlers, owned property along this street. Only one cutler was present north of the river, while in the south of the city they were found only in the sub-leets of St Peter Mancroft and St Andrew. The three individuals present in St Peter Mancroft were all buying and selling shops, while those elsewhere were concerned with land and messuages.

Five lorimers (or harness makers) are present in the deed sample holding land in the sub-leets of St Giles, Berstrete, St Stephen and St Peter Mancroft. There are records of a similar number of latoners, who were concerned with the manufacture of monumental brasses and church furnishings from latten, an alloy of copper and other metals. Not surprisingly, they were found within easy reach of ecclesiastical centres: the Cathedral, the Dominican friary, the Chapel-in-the-Field in St Stephen's parish, and also in St Peter Mancroft. The locative surname of two of them, de York, suggests that they had migrated from another important cathedral city.

CLOTHING

Those engaged in the manufacture of clothing make up 5% of the known-trade population. This group comprises fifteen tailors, fifteen glovers, nine hatters, nine hosiers and four girdlers. Although these numbers are small, it is possible to discern distribution patterns in their property interests. The tailors and hosiers, for instance (of whom little else can be said), were scattered throughout the city, and were the only representatives of this trade group to hold property north of the river. In contrast, the glovers, hatters and girdlers seem to have had property interests in specific localities. No representative of the clothing group was found among the population of South Conesford.

The fifteen recorded glovers seem to have been located where they could easily obtain supplies of their raw materials. Eleven individuals held property in Berstrete sub-leet, and three were found not far away in the sub-leet of St Giles. (The fifth is not located in a parish.) Berstrete was conveniently near the butchers, who were also concentrated in this area, and from whom they were no doubt buying skins. Most stages in the processing of leather[75] were thus present in Berstrete by c. 1300: a situation similar to that identified by Phythian-Adams in 16th-century Coventry where 'the secondary occupations in industrial terms - the corvisors and glovers, for instance - were sited in relation to the primary producers, the tanners and whittawers'.[76]

The nine hatters recorded in the deeds were all grouped in the sub-leets of St Peter Mancroft and St Andrew, presumably attracted by the proximity of the market. The four recorded girdlers also seem to be grouped around the market, in the sub-leets of St Peter Mancroft, St Stephen and St Giles. Hosiers, however, do not seem to have been confined to a particular area, and were active in six of the eleven sub-leets. Their transactions generally concerned messuages with buildings and land, but also, in St Giles, involved land with tenter-grounds and a frame.

BUILDING TRADES

Workers in the building trades, comprising fourteen masons, ten carpenters, seven painters, two roofers, one plumber and one limeworker, form only 4% of the known-trade population. There was no apparent zoning of these trades, and representatives were to be found in every sub-leet in the city, with the exception of St Stephen.

Although the largest group of masons held property north of the river in the sub-leet of St Clement Fyebridge, there were others in St Giles, St Stephen and South Conesford. In North Conesford a minor concentration of four masons is perhaps best explained by the proximity of the cathedral. The limited scattering of masons throughout the city probably reflects the paucity of domestic stone-built structures in the early-14th-century town, but it is likely that the renewal and repair of the parish churches would have provided a continuous, if small-scale, opportunity for employment. Unlike the situation in Winchester,[77] there is no indication that many of the Norwich masons were temporary residents in the city, for throughout the twenty-six year period only one man, Robert de Novo Castro subter Lymen, bought and subsequently sold the same property,[78] and this transaction probably arose from his marriage to the widow who formerly owned it. The existence of migrant masons who may only have been tenants of houses would not, of course, be documented in the deeds. The Freemen's Rolls suggest that the number of masons in the city was to remain low, with on average five admissions per annum, until 1440, when the average rose to ten, the newcomers perhaps attracted by the massive 15th-century reconstruction of the Norwich churches.[79]

The ten carpenters were dispersed throughout seven of the sub-leets of the city, with no evident concentration in any particular area. They were absent from St George Tombland, North Conesford, St Peter Mancroft and St Stephen. Their transactions were all concerned with land, rents and messuages, with the one exception of the selling by John Cok and his wife Margaret of three shops cum fundo in the parish of St Saviour in St Clement Fyebridge sub-leet.

There is, therefore, no indication of grouping by workers in the building trade in particular areas of the city, although the Cathedral may possibly have provided a focus for the activities of the masons.

AGRICULTURAL TRADES

In spite of the small numbers involved, it is still worth stressing that some of the city inhabitants had agricultural connections. There are, for instance, two referred to as messor, an 'overseer of harvest' or 'hayward'. Their names, John de Martham and Galf de Wyketoft, suggest that they (or their predecessors) originated from villages in the county, or it may perhaps be that it was there that they practised their agricultural occupations. Another example is the shepherd, Roger le Quite, who bought a messuage with buildings in St Augustine's parish in the north of the city.[80] This was an underdeveloped area of the city where a shepherd might easily find employment, or, alternatively, nearby Mousehold Heath may well have provided opportunities for pastoral employment.

SERVICE TRADES

The deeds record nine individuals in five different occupations who offered services to the population of early-14th-century Norwich. There were three barbers, three physicians, one surgeon, one scriptor (scrivenor) and one brevitor (letter-writer). Their property interests, as might be expected, were not confined to any particular area, but were scattered throughout the city. The barbers were concerned with messuages in the sub-leets of St Stephen, St Peter Mancroft and St George Tombland, while the physicians held property interests in those of St Clement Fyebridge, Berstrete and South Conesford. Ralph de Morlee, the only surgeon, appears in the deeds quitclaiming rights to a messuage in St Peter Parmountergate.[81] The scrivenor and the letter-writer both provided a service of the same kind as that offered by the clerks (see p.19) and were found in St George Tombland and St Peter Parmountergate.

MISCELLANEOUS

The remaining occupations recorded in the deeds have been grouped together in a 'miscellaneous' section. This includes: chandlers (four), coopers (three), boatmen (three), perfumerers (two), a pursemaker, a turner, a sergeant, a carter and one fletcher. As far as it is possible to tell from such small numbers, these trades were grouped in particular areas. The chandlers were found in the sub-leets of St Stephen and Berstrete, presumably because of the presence in the latter of the butchers from whom they obtained their raw material; the boatmen were present near the river in both St George Tombland and South Conesford; and the cooper, turner and fletcher, all working with wood, held land in St Andrew sub-leet. The perfumerers, who were catering for the luxury end of the retail trade, were found, not surprisingly, in the market area of St Peter Mancroft parish; while the pursemaker can be associated with the other secondary occupations of the leather trade such as glovers, in Berstrete.

CONCLUSION

The deed evidence can provide only an incomplete impression of the trade structure and economy of Norwich c. 1300, but it is clear that in common with other pre-industrial towns,[82] the city had not yet developed a specialised economy: industry, commerce, services and even, to a certain extent, agricultural pursuits were important to the city. A high percentage of the population was concerned with manufacturing finished articles from various different raw materials, and such manufacturers were not only producing staples such as clothes and shoes, but also specialist luxuries like jewellery, parchment and armour. The city would thus have catered not only for its own more everyday needs but also would have served as a centre for the surrounding area of rural villages and smaller market towns. The high number of merchants present in the city would have been attracted by the opportunity to trade on a large scale and in turn were likely to have provided capital to stimulate economic activity.

The processing of raw materials, whether wool, leather or metal was clearly of as much importance as the manufacturing and distribution of finished articles. Dyers, fullers and shearmen were all involved in the manufacturing of the cloth made up by the tailors or sold by the drapers; while tanners, skinners and tawyers worked the hides provided by the butchers and made up by the shoemakers, saddlers and glovers. The picture is one of an integrated industrial society where raw materials provided or initially processed by some trades were worked up further by others and then distributed.

Although the textile industry was to dominate the city's economy from the 15th century onwards, at the end of the 13th century this and the leather industry were of almost equal importance; both were well-established and between them accounted for over a quarter of the known-trade population. A primary requirement for the processing of both leather and the fulling and dyeing of cloth was a good water supply, and workers in these trades held property along either bank of the river in the west of the city.

The distribution of members of the provisioning trades such as tavernkeepers, cooks, fishermen and poulterers give an indication of the early importance of St George Tombland as a provisioning centre of the city, providing a possible alternative to the market in St Peter Mancroft. Fishermen added to the congestion of the river frontage in the west of the city, but, apart from isolated examples, are not recorded in the deeds for Conesford. Bakers were scattered throughout the city but were also concentrated in St Peter Mancroft and St Gregory within easy reach of the market place. On several occasions bakeries are recorded as being in the possession of merchants, who could provide the substantial capital required for the purchase of ovens and who were likely to be buying them for investment purposes.

The greatest variety of metal trades was found centred on the market parish of St Peter Mancroft, where the goldsmiths, the lorimers and the one armourer were probably catering for the luxury end of the market. Smiths, however, were concentrated in the north of the city, presumably for reasons of safety and to minimise the risk of fire. Building workers and those engaged in the service trades seem to have been scattered throughout the city, although their numbers were greater in the south than the north.

Norwich merchants were apparently disinclined to invest in

property in the northern part of the city: only two properties in St Michael Coslany and three in St Clement Fyebridge were in their possession in contrast to greater numbers in the more highly-developed and presumably more prosperous area of the south-west. Their involvement in different types of property - tentergrounds, kilns, bakeries, fish-houses and barns - suggest that their wealth was accumulated by means of a diversity of interests.

The ecclesiastics recorded in the deeds were also investing in a variety of types of property - chaplains and clerks as well as rectors, vicars and parsons were sufficiently affluent to own land. In contrast to the merchants, however, they were present in greatest numbers in those areas of the city that were under-exploited by other trade groups, namely, St Michael Coslany and St Clement north of the river, and the eastern sub-leets of South and North Conesford.

Although there seems to have been no marked zoning of occupations in Norwich, different parts of the city may have had particular characteristics. The relative absence of industrial activity in Conesford was probably the result of some degree of monopolisation of the area by a number of wealthy families and religious institutions. The precincts of the Franciscan and Austin friars were in this area and officials from the Cathedral and abbeys from further afield held interests here also. Even the city's common staithe, situated further south in Conesford, was rented from the Prior of Wendling. The overall impression is that this was primarily the wealthy residential area of the city.

There was also an apparent localisation of leather workers in the sub-leet of Berstrete, where butchers, skinners and glovers, representing three different stages in the processing of leather, were concentrated. The presence of butchers in Berstrete was one of the most enduring features of the city topography: they were well-established by 1300 and survived into the 20th century, no doubt because this area lay between the cattle market to the north and grazing lands to the south.

The most striking industrial concentration was that of the dyers in the parish of St Lawrence. This marked grouping in such a small area is unusual at this period in the city. There may have been earlier trade zoning as suggested by the street names of Pottergate and Fishergate but they have disappeared by the late 13th century.

Norwich at this period was thus prosperous and populous; it was reacting to and coping with an expanding population by extending the built-up area; and the deeds illustrate not only an active market in land but also the rich variety of trades practised within the city.

CAPTIONS TO TABLES 1-3, WHICH APPEAR OVERLEAF

Table 1

Percentage of individuals in each occupation holding property in one or more parish (1% of the merchants held property in 12 parishes).

Table 2

Breakdown by sub-leet of the distribution of trades-interests e.g. of the 61 tanners' interests, 2 (or 3%), were in South Conesford. Percentages are italicised.

Table 3

Percentage breakdown by occupation and trade group of the distribution of trades-interest e.g. 4% of those in South Conesford were tanners'. The trade group totals, those plotted on Fig. 3, were calculated independently.

Number of parishes	1	2	3	4	5	6	7	8	South Conesford		North Conesford		Berstrete		St Stephen		Peter Mancroft		St Giles		St Gregory		St Andrew		St George Tombland		St Michael Coslany		St Clement Fyebridge		South Conesford	North Conesford	Berstrete	St Stephen	Peter Mancroft	St Giles	St Gregory	St Andrew	St George Tombland	St Michael Coslany	St Clement Fyebridge	
LEATHER																																										LEATHER
Tanners	82	11	4	2	-	-	-	2	2	3	0	16	2	3	2	3	5	8	6	10	1	2	3	5	1	2	15	25	14	23	4	21	1	2	3	5	1	2	1	13	12	Tanners
Skinners	85	12	3	-	-	-	-	-	1	3	2	5	9	24	4	11	5	13	4	11	1	3	4	11	-		4	11	4	11	2	4	6	4	3	3	1	3	-	3	3	Skinners
Tawyers	82	18	-	-	-	-	-	-	-		-		1	5	4	20	7	35	3	15	2	10	2	10	-		-		1	5	-	-	1	4	4	2	2	2	-	-	1	Tawyers
Whitawers	100	-	-	-	-	-	-	-	-		-		-		-		-		2	100	-		-		-		-		-		-	-	-	-	-	2	-	-	-	-	-	Whitawers
Shoemakers	86	7	2	4	2	-	-	-	-		-		8	12	4	6	10	15	9	13	4	6	18	26	2	3	10	15	4	6	-	-	5	4	6	7	3	14	3	9	3	Shoemakers
Saddlers	88	13	-	-	-	-	-	-	-		-		4	44	-		4	44	1	11	-		-		-		-		-		-	-	3	-	2	1	-	-	-	-	-	Saddlers
Parchmentmakers	100	-	-	-	-	-	-	-	-		-		-		-		-		-		-		2	67	-		1	33	-		-	-	-	-	-	-	-	2	-	1	-	Parchmentmakers
									3		12		24		14		31		25		8		29		3		30		23		6	26	16	15	19	20	7	22	4	26	19	
TEXTILES																																										TEXTILES
Drapers	74	15	9	-	-	3	-	-	3	7	1	2	1	2	6	13	8	18	8	18	2	4	4	9	2	4	6	13	4	9	6	2	1	7	5	7	2	3	3	5	3	Drapers
Linendrapers	77	19	4	-	-	-	-	-	-		-		6	18	5	15	8	24	7	21	2	6	3	9	-		2	6	1	3	-	-	4	5	5	6	2	2	-	2	1	Linendrapers
Woolmen	45	45	9	-	-	-	-	-	1	6	1	6	2	13	-		2	13	2	13	5	31	1	6	-		1	6	1	6	2	2	1	-	1	2	4	1	-	1	1	Woolmen
Dyers	67	23	7	3	-	-	-	-	1	3	-		1	3	1	3	1	3	7	18	20	50	1	3	-		8	20	-		2	-	1	1	1	6	17	1	-	7	-	Dyers
Fullers	90	10	-	-	-	-	-	-	-		-		-		-		1	9	2	18	4	36	2	18	-		2	18	-		-	-	-	-	1	2	3	2	-	2	-	Fullers
Weavers	93	7	-	-	-	-	-	-	-		-		-		1	7	-		-		4	27	6	40	-		1	7	3	20	-	-	-	1	-	-	3	5	-	1	3	Weavers
Shearmen	71	29	-	-	-	-	-	-	-		-		1	11	-		-		1	11	6	67	-		-		1	11	-		-	-	1	-	-	1	5	-	-	1	-	Shearmen
Flaxmen	100	-	-	-	-	-	-	-	-		-		-		-		-		1	100	-		-		-		-		-		-	-	-	-	-	1	-	-	-	-	-	Flaxmen
Woadmerchants	100	-	-	-	-	-	-	-	-		-		-		-		-		2	22	2	22	-		-		3	34	2	22	-	-	-	-	-	2	2	-	-	3	2	Woadmerchants
Quilters	100	-	-	-	-	-	-	-	-		-		1	50	-		-		1	50	-		-		-		-		-		-	-	1	-	-	1	-	-	-	-	-	Quilters
									5		2		12		13		20		31		45		17		2		24		11		10	4	8	14	12	25	39	13	' 3	21	9	
CLOTHING																																										CLOTHING
Tailors	73	27	-	-	-	-	-	-	-		2	10	2	10	2	10	1	5	1	5	2	10	2	10	3	15	2	10	3	15	-	4	1	2	1	1	2	2	4	2	3	Tailors
Hatters	100	-	-	-	-	-	-	-	-		-		-		-		6	67	-		-		3	33	-		-		-		-	-	-	-	4	-	-	2	-	-	-	Hatters
Hosiers	89	11	-	-	-	-	-	-	-		-		1	11	1	11	1	11	2	22	-		3	33	-		1	11	-		-	-	1	1	1	2	-	2	-	1	-	Hosiers
Glovers	77	23	-	-	-	-	-	-	-		-		11	73	-		-		4	27	-		-		-		-		-		-	-	7	-	-	3	-	-	-	-	-	Glovers
Girdlers	100	-	-	-	-	-	-	-	-		-		-		1	25	2	50	1	25	-		-		-		-		-		-	-	-	1	1	1	-	-	-	-	-	Girdlers
											2		14		4		10		8		2		8		3		3		3			4	9	4	6	7	2	6	4	3	3	
METAL																																										METAL
Cutlers	83	17	-	-	-	-	-	-	-		-		-		-		5	56	-		-		3	33	-		-		1	11	-	-	-	-	3	-	-	2	-	-	1	Cutlers
Goldsmiths	94	6	-	-	-	-	-	-	-		-		2	11	-		7	37	3	16	1	5	4	21	2	11	-		-		-	-	1	-	4	2	1	3	3	-	-	Goldsmiths
Furbishers	100	-	-	-	-	-	-	-	-		-		-		-		1	50	-		-		1	50	-		-		-		-	-	-	-	1	-	-	1	-	-	-	Furbishers
Lorimers	80	20	-	-	-	-	-	-	-		-		1	17	1	17	3	50	1	17	-		-		-		-		-		-	-	1	1	2	1	-	-	-	-	-	Lorimers
Latoners	75	25	-	-	-	-	-	-	-		1	17	-		1	17	3	50	-		-		1	17	-		-		-		-	2	-	1	2	-	-	1	-	-	-	Latoners
Armourers	-	100	-	-	-	-	-	-	-		-		1	50	-		1	50	-		-		-		-		-		-		-	-	1	-	1	-	-	-	-	-	-	Armourers
Smiths	94	6	-	-	-	-	-	-	-		-		-		2	12	-		2	12	-		5	29	1	6	-		7	41	-	-	-	2	-	2	-	4	1	-	6	Smiths
Needlers	100	-	-	-	-	-	-	-	-		1	50	1	50	-		-		-		-		-		-		-		-		-	2	1	-	-	-	-	-	-	-	-	Needlers
Bellfounders	100	-	-	-	-	-	-	-	-		-		-		-		-		-		-		-		2	100	-		-		-	-	-	-	-	-	-	-	2	-	-	Bellfounders
											2		5		4		20		6		1		14		5				8			4	3	4	12	5	1	11	7		7	
PROVISIONS																																										PROVISIONS
Butchers	71	30	-	-	-	-	-	-	-		-		9	43	5	24	6	29	-		-		1	5	-		-		-		-	-	6	5	4	-	-	1	-	-	-	Butchers
Bakers	88	9	-	2	-	-	-	-	2	4	-		5	10	9	19	6	13	4	8	10	21	2	4	4	8	4	8	2	4	4	-	3	10	4	3	9	2	5	3	2	Bakers
Fishers	82	13	5	-	-	-	-	-	2	5	-		-		-		4	9	7	16	7	16	4	9	9	20	8	18	3	7	4	-	-	-	2	6	6	3	12	7	3	Fishers
Cooks	100	-	-	-	-	-	-	-	-		-		-		-		-		-		-		1	14	4	57	-		2	29	-	-	-	-	-	-	-	1	5	-	2	Cooks
Poulterers	75	25	-	-	-	-	-	-	1	17	-		1	17	-		2	33	-		-		-		2	33	-		-		2	-	1	-	1	-	-	-	3	-	-	Poulterers

Limeworker	100	–	–	–	–	–	–	–
SERVICES								
Surgeons	100	–	–	–	–	–	–	–
Doctors	–	100	–	–	–	–	–	–
Barbers	100	–	–	–	–	–	–	–
Scriptors	100	–	–	–	–	–	–	–
Brevitors	100	–	–	–	–	–	–	–
MERCANTILE								
Merchants	66	22	4	4	1	–	2	–
AGRICULTURAL								
Messors	100	–	–	–	–	–	–	–
Shepherds	100	–	–	–	–	–	–	–
ECCLESIASTICAL								
Chaplains	83	13	2	2	–	–	–	–
Clerks	81	12	–	4	–	–	3	–
Rectors	84	10	7	–	–	–	–	–
Parsons	100	–	–	–	–	–	–	–
Vicars	100	–	–	–	–	–	–	–
Anchorites	100	–	–	–	–	–	–	–
MISCELLANEOUS								
Pursemakers	100	–	–	–	–	–	–	–
Perfumerers	100	–	–	–	–	–	–	–
Chandlers	75	25	–	–	–	–	–	–
Coopers	100	–	–	–	–	–	–	–
Turners	100	–	–	–	–	–	–	–
Boatmen	100	–	–	–	–	–	–	–
Serjeants	100	–	–	–	–	–	–	–
Carters	100	–	–	–	–	–	–	–
Fletcher	100	–	–	–	–	–	–	–

Limeworker	–	–	1 100	–	–	–	–	–	–	–	–
	2	4	9		2	1	3	3	3	4	7
SERVICES											
Surgeons	–	1 100	–	–	–	–	–	–	–	–	–
Doctors	1 25	–	1 25	–	–	–	–	–	–	–	2 50
Barbers	–	–	–	1 33	1 33	–	–	–	1 33	–	–
Scriptors	–	1 100	–	–	–	–	–	–	–	–	–
Brevitors	–	–	–	–	–	–	–	–	1 100	–	–
	1	2	1	1	1				2		2
MERCANTILE											
Merchants	5 3	8 5	14 9	20 13	34 22	20 13	20 13	20 13	5 3	1 1	5 3
	5	8	14	20	34	20	20	20	5	1	5
AGRICULTURAL											
Messors	–	1 50	–	–	–	–	1 50	–	–	–	–
Shepherds	–	–	–	–	–	–	–	–	–	–	1 100
		1					1				1
ECCLESIASTICAL											
Chaplains	12 8	7 5	27 19	9 6	11 8	7 5	7 5	13 9	9 6	15 10	25 18
Clerks	10 11	2 2	12 13	6 6	7 8	8 9	5 5	8 9	8 9	16 17	11 12
Rectors	7 18	1 3	1 3	1 3	–	5 13	3 8	5 13	2 5	6 15	8 21
Parsons	1 7	2 14	–	1 7	–	1 7	2 14	1 7	1 7	1 7	4 29
Vicars	–	1 33	–	–	–	–	–	–	1 33	–	1 33
Anchorites	–	–	1 25	–	–	–	–	–	–	2 50	1 25
	30	13	41	17	18	21	17	27	21	40	50
MISCELLANEOUS											
Pursemakers	–	–	1 100	–	–	–	–	–	–	–	–
Perfumerers	–	–	–	–	2 100	–	–	–	–	–	–
Chandlers	–	–	3 60	1 20	–	–	–	–	1 20	–	–
Coopers	–	–	2 67	–	–	–	–	1 33	–	–	–
Turners	–	–	–	–	–	–	–	1 100	–	–	–
Boatmen	1 33	–	–	–	–	–	–	–	2 67	–	–
Serjeants	–	–	1 100	–	–	–	–	–	–	–	–
Carters	–	–	1 100	–	–	–	–	–	–	–	–
Fletcher	–	–	–	–	–	–	–	1 100	–	–	–
	1		8	1	2			3	3		
Total trades-interests (1172)	52	46	148	91	162	123	115	129	73	115	118
Total Deed Popn. (3851)	230	190	496	311	479	382	312	386	247	390	428

–	–	1	–	–	–	–	–	–	–	–	Limeworker
4	9	7		1	1	3	2	4	3	6	
											SERVICES
–	2	–	–	–	–	–	–	–	–	–	Surgeons
2	–	1	–	–	–	–	–	–	–	2	Doctors
–	–	–	1	1	–	–	–	1	–	–	Barbers
–	2	–	–	–	–	–	–	–	–	–	Scriptors
–	–	–	–	–	–	–	–	1	–	–	Brevitors
2	4	1	1	1				3		2	
											MERCANTILE
10	17	9	22	21	16	17	16	7	1	4	Merchants
10	17	9	22	21	16	17	16	7	1	4	
											AGRICULTURAL
–	2	–	–	–	–	1	–	–	–	–	Messors
–	–	–	–	–	–	–	–	–	–	1	Shepherds
–	2					1				1	
											ECCLESIASTICAL
23	15	18	9	7	6	6	10	12	13	21	Chaplains
19	4	8	7	4	7	4	6	11	14	9	Clerks
13	2	1	1	–	4	3	4	3	5	7	Rectors
2	4	–	1	–	1	2	1	1	1	3	Parsons
–	2	–	–	–	–	–	–	1	–	1	Vicars
–	–	1	–	–	–	–	–	–	2	1	Anchorites
58	28	28	19	11	17	15	21	29	35	42	
											MISCELLANEOUS
–	–	1	–	–	–	–	–	–	–	–	Pursemakers
–	–	–	–	1	–	–	–	–	–	–	Perfumerers
–	–	2	1	–	–	–	–	1	–	–	Chandlers
–	–	1	–	–	–	–	1	–	–	–	Coopers
–	–	–	–	–	–	–	1	–	–	–	Turners
2	–	–	–	–	–	–	–	3	–	–	Boatmen
–	–	–	–	–	–	–	–	–	–	–	Serjeants
–	–	1	–	–	–	–	–	–	–	–	Carters
–	–	–	–	–	–	–	1	–	–	–	Fletchers
2		5	1	1			2	4			

Table 1

Multiple ownership of property

Table 2

Trades-interests by sub-leet

Table 3

The numerical basis for Fig.3

ENDNOTES

1. Norfolk Record Office, Norwich City Records, case 1, shelf a, Court Rolls 1-5. (hereafter, references to the court rolls will give roll and membrane numbers only). These rolls cover the period 1285 to 1311 and references to c. 1300 in the text are used as a shorthand notation for this date bracket.

2. D.M. Woodward, 'Sources for Urban History, Freemen's Rolls', The Local Historian 9, No.2, 1970, pp.89-94.

3. Also excluded from this study are those individuals who were solely concerned with property in the city market and all those who may appear on the court rolls for reasons other than to enrol property interests. For example, the information contained in wills recorded on the rolls has not been taken into account.

4. R. McKinley, Norfolk and Suffolk Surnames in the Middle Ages (English Surnames Series II, London 1975), pp.52-4.

5. See p.65 below.

6. J. Campbell, Norwich (fascicle of the Historic Town Plans Atlas, London 1975), p.10.

7. The term 'citizen' is used here in the sense of inhabitant, rather than in its more precise legal sense. A cursory check through the computer printout for explicit mention of citizenship reveals that less than 500 of those recorded in the deeds (approximately 4,000 individuals) are referred to as such. This would suggest that this distinction was not considered important in Norwich c. 1300, at least not in the process of enrolment of property interests. See, however, W. Hudson, 'Notes about Norwich before the close of the thirteenth century', Norfolk Archaeology XII, 1895, pp.25-84.

8. See pp.54 and 64 below.

9. The ambiguities of by-name evidence are stressed by the fact that approximately 50 trades or occupations not recorded in the deeds appear as by-names. If, however, these were hereditary there is no reason to believe that they were practised in Norwich.

10. Details of the methodology adopted, computer programs run and the code book used for abbreviations are available, together with details of the archive, from the Centre of East Anglian Studies, UEA, Norwich.

11. W. Hudson and J.C. Tingey (eds.) The Records of the City of Norwich (Norwich 1906), I, pp.xxvii-xxciii. Unqualified references in the text to e.g. St Stephen are to the sub-leet not the parish.

12. Roll 2, m.37d. Unless so qualified membrane references are to recto.

13. Cf. the position in early-16th-century Lincolnshire. D. Owen, Church and Society in Medieval Lincolnshire (History of Lincolnshire V, Lincoln 1971), p.133.

14. F. Blomefield, The History of the City and County of Norwich, (London 1806), I, pp.74-5.

15. C. Platt, The Parish Churches of Medieval England, (London 1981), pp.52-3.

16. P. Heath, The Parish Clergy on the Eve of the Reformation, (London 1969), p.19.

17. Roll 1, m.2d.

18. Rolls 2, m.41 and 4, m.27.

19. Roll 4, m.27d.

20. Roll 3, m.2.

21. Roll 2, m.27d.

22. Roll 4, m.11d.

23. Roll 4, m.20.

24. Roll 2, m.23.

25. J. Kirkpatrick, History of the Religious Orders and Communities and of the Hospitals and Castle of Norwich, (London 1845), p.2.

26. For the Dominicans see Roll 5, m.23; for the Franciscans Roll 3, m.10d; and for the Austin Friars Roll 2, m.25.

27. Roll 4, m.24d.

28. Roll 1, m.1d.

29. Roll 4, m.33d.

30. Calendar of Patent Rolls Edward I (1292-1301), (London 1895), p.14.

31. Roll 2, m.41.

32. Dr Dyson has, anyway, suggested that many quays or staithes are no more than riverside reclamations or revetments: A.G. Dyson, 'The terms "quay" and "wharf" and the early medieval London waterfront' in G. Milne and B. Hobley (eds.) Waterfront Archaeology in Britain and Northern Europe (Council for British Archaeology Research Report 41, London 1981), p.38.

33. Roll 2, mm.10 and 8d; Roll 5, m.23.

34. A.G. Dyson 'The terms "quay" and "wharf" ...', p.38.

35. A. Carter, 'Norwich' in G. Milne and B. Hobley (eds.) Waterfront Archaeology ..., p.139.

36. W. Hudson and J.C. Tingey (eds.) The Records of the City of Norwich (Norwich 1910), II, pp.233-6.

37. For de Freston see Roll 2, m.30; for Woburn and Garendon see notes 29 and 30 above; for Wendling see Roll 4, m.11d.

38. F.M. Powicke, The Thirteenth Century 1216-1307, (London 1953), p.663.

39. J. Kirkpatrick, Streets and Lanes of the City of Norwich, written c. 1725, ed. W. Hudson, (Norwich 1889), p.16, also Campbell, Norwich, Map 2.

40. Campbell, Norwich, p.25.

41. Kirkpatrick, Streets and Lanes ..., p.27.

42. As with other streets e.g. Pottergate, the formation of the name could date from a period well before it is first recorded. Pers.comm. Karl Inge Sandred.

43. Kirkpatrick, Streets and Lanes ..., p.88, and Campbell, Norwich, Map 2.

44. C. Platt, The English Medieval Town, (London 1976), p.47.

45. Kirkpatrick, Streets and Lanes ..., p.41 fn.8 and p.3.

46. E.M. Veale, English Fur Trade in the Later Middle Ages, (Oxford 1966), p.50.

47. Acts of the Privy Council, 1616-17, p.168, quoted in E.M. Veale, English Fur Trade ..., p.26.

48. Campbell, Norwich, p.16.

49. Kirkpatrick, Streets and Lanes ..., p.52.

50. A. Carter and J.P. Roberts, 'Excavations in Norwich 1972. The Norwich Survey - Second Interim Report' Norfolk Archaeology, XXV, pt.iv, 1973, pp.461-2 and 466-7.

51. Roll 4, m.23d.

52. Hudson and Tingey, Records ... of Norwich, II, p.312

53. Blomefield, History of ... Norwich, p.78.

54. Kirkpatrick, Streets and Lanes ..., p.21.

55. Kirkpatrick, Streets and Lanes ..., p.55.

56. Pers.comm. the late Helen Sutermeister.

57. Kirkpatrick, Streets and Lanes ..., p.54.

58. Kirkpatrick, Streets and Lanes ..., p.58.

59. W. Hudson (ed.), Leet Jurisdiction in the City of Norwich during the XIIIth and XIVth Centuries, (Selden Society V, London 1891), p.31.

60. Campbell, Norwich, p.11.

61. F. Bond, Dedications and Patron Saints of English Churches, Ecclesiastical Symbolism, Saints and their Emblems, (London 1914), p.136. 'S. Bartholomew is recorded to have been flayed alive, and is represented with a flaying knife in his hand, and sometimes with his skin over his arm, as on the bronze grille round the tomb of King Henry VII in Westminster Abbey'.

62. The church, and presumably its dedication, like the nearby St John de Sepulchre, probably dates from before 1100: E.M. Jope, 'Excavations in the City of Norwich, 1948', Norfolk Archaeology, XXX, pt.iv, 1952, p.320.

63. Kirkpatrick, Streets and Lanes ..., p.65.

64. Blomefield, History of ... Norwich, II, p.326.

65. Roll 4, m.4d.

66. Kirkpatrick, Streets and Lanes ..., p.67.

67. Campbell, Norwich, p.13.

68. Pers.comm. Robert Smith, Buildings Group, Norwich Survey.

69. Campbell, *Norwich*, p.13.

70. W. Urry, *Canterbury under the Angevins*, (London 1967), p.112.

71. M.W. Atkin and A. Carter, 'Excavations in Norwich 1976/7. The Norwich Survey - Sixth Interim Report', *Norfolk Archaeology*, XXXVI, 1977, p.289, and M.W. Atkin and H. Sutermeister, 'Excavations in Norwich 1977/8. The Norwich Survey - Seventh Interim Report', *Norfolk Archaeology*, XXXVII, 1978, p.20.

72. Poem, pre-1450,written on a blank folio of a 13th-century Norwich Cathedral Priory manuscript (now BL MS Arundel 292) quoted by Elizabeth Salter, 'A Complaint against Blacksmiths', *Literature and History*, 5:2, Autumn 1979, p.194.

73. H. Clarke and A. Carter, *Excavations in King's Lynn 1968-70*, (Society for Medieval Archaeology monograph, London 1977), pp.425 and 442.

74. Kirkpatrick, *Streets and Lanes ...*, p.43.

75. No tradesmen dressing skins for the glovers were recorded here.

76. C. Phythian-Adams, *Desolation of a City, Coventry and the Urban Crisis of the Late Middle Ages*, (Cambridge 1979), p.161.

77. D. Keene, 'Some Aspects of the History, Topography and Archaeology of the North-Eastern Part of the Medieval City of Winchester with special reference to the Brooks Area', unpublished D.Phil thesis, University of Oxford.

78. Roll 2, mm.20d and 24d.

79. Blomefield, *History of ... Norwich*, II *passim*.

80. Roll 5, m.1d.

81. Roll 2, m.20d.

82. C. Phythian-Adams, 'The Economic and Social Structure' in *The Fabric of the Traditional Community*, (The Open University, English Urban History 1500-1700, A322 Unit 5, Milton Keynes 1977), p.15.

PROPERTY TRANSFER AND ENROLMENT IN NORWICH 1285—1311

by

Elizabeth Rutledge

INTRODUCTION

The object in undertaking this study was, firstly, to examine the nature of enrolment and of the documents enrolled to see whether, and to what extent, this might affect work based on the rolls; and, secondly, to discover what was happening to property interests in Norwich. This paper concentrates on the first five rolls, dating from July 1285 to October 1311, which were used in the computer project.[1] In particular, two five-year periods (July 1285 to May 1290 and October 1306 to October 1311) have been looked at in detail, to see if there were any changes in the composition of the rolls. These dates may seem arbitrary, and require some explanation. The first period ends in May 1290 because from then until March 1291, the dates of individual courts are not entered and the deeds can only be dated by year. The second period ends in October 1311 because Roll 5 contains one entry for October. October cannot be said to be covered, however, as Roll 6 begins with another ten entries for the same month.

Also used in the reconstructions, though not in the computer program, were original deeds (usually known as Private Deeds[2]), relating to property in Norwich from among the Norwich city records. These came into the hands of the city in a number of different ways. Some may have been brought to the city court to be acknowledged and/ or enrolled, or as evidence in a dispute and never reclaimed; others concern property owned by the city or agreements made by its officials, while a few were simply given to the city at a much later date by private individuals, and placed with the rest. These original deeds are arranged according to the parish in which the property they transfer lies. In this paper they are used mainly to help explain the process of enrolment. A few of the many deeds relating to Norwich properties from among the records of the Dean and Chapter of Norwich have been used for the same purpose.[3]

1. ENROLMENT

a) THE COURT ROLLS

The series of Norwich city court rolls begins in July 1285.[4] The first roll is headed 'Roll of charters recognised in the full court of Norwich produced (traditarum) and in the same court endorsed beginning on the Wednesday next after the feast of the apostles Peter and Paul in the thirteenth year of the reign of King Edward' (4 July 1285). Similar headings recur throughout the rolls. It is therefore clear from the beginning that these rolls were limited to enrolments, and were not part of a series of rolls on which general court business was entered, such as survive at, for example, Great

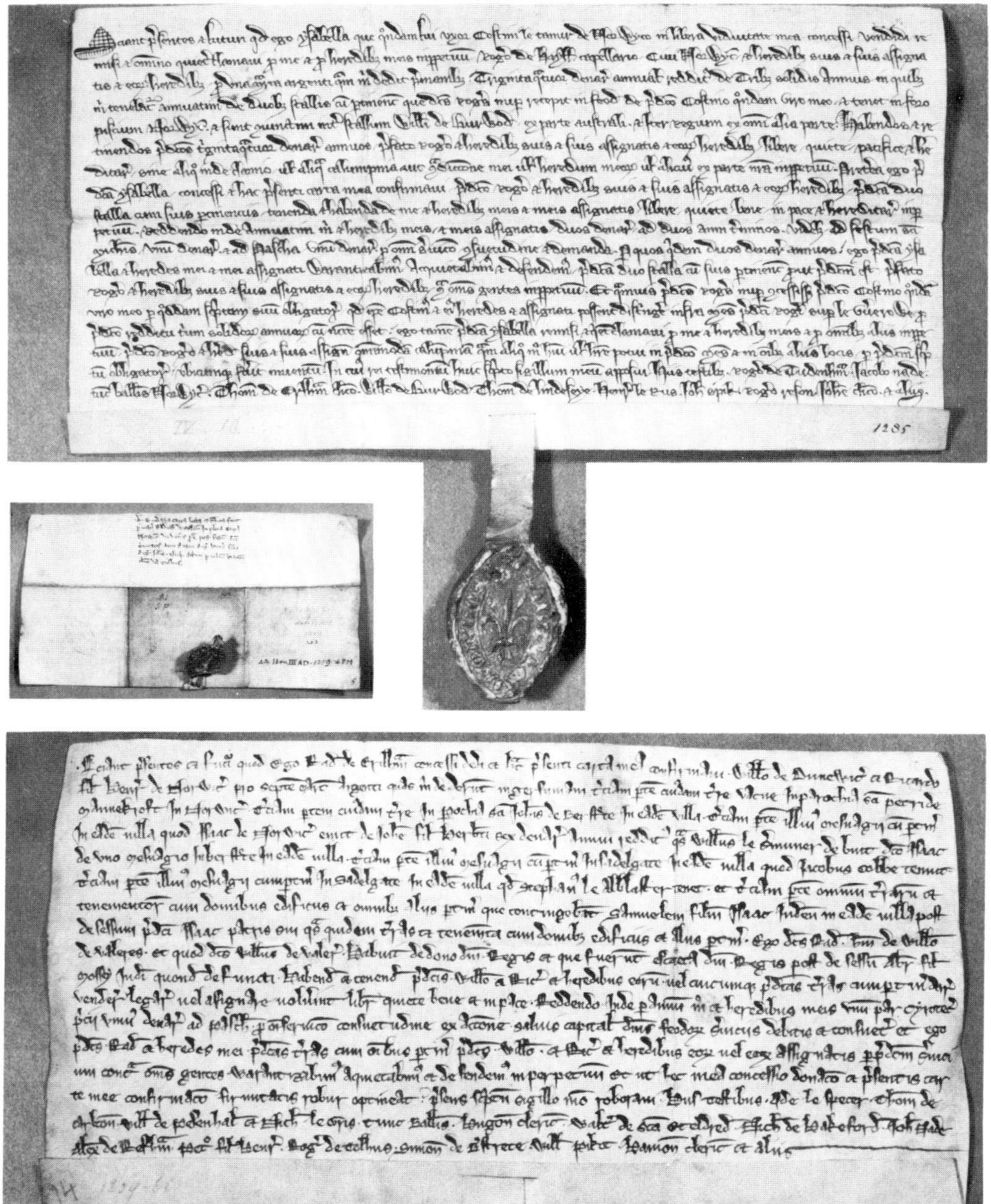

Pl.2

Two original deeds (PD, St Peter Mancroft, 1280-89 and 1260-69). Note the difference in handwriting between the upper, written by John, and the lower written by Hamon. In both documents the clerk's name appears four words from the end of the deed at the end of the witness list. Inset at small scale is the endorsed reverse of the lower deed.

Yarmouth and Colchester.[5] Deeds were certainly being acknowledged in the city court of Norwich before the surviving court rolls begin. Among the City Private Deeds are a grant and a quitclaim endorsed (written on the back) with memoranda that they were 'read and produced/delivered (tradita) in the full court of Norwich' as early as 1250 and 1253.[6] This is not exceptional. Transfers of property were noted at Wallingford as early as 1232/3; there was a separate roll for recognizances of deeds in the hustings court of London by 1252; and there are similar acknowledgements in the Ipswich general court rolls of 1255.[7] However, though it is not unlikely that enrolments were also made in Norwich before 1285, either on a general court roll or on an earlier roll of the existing series, these endorsements do not prove this.[8] Even after 1285 deeds could be recognised before the court and endorsed without being enrolled, and the later enrolment of several deeds drawn up before 1285 might suggest that it was not possible to enrol them at the date they were written (see p.50).

The earliest Norwich court roll consists of three membranes sewn together at the top, the first two membranes themselves each consisting of four pieces of parchment stitched head to tail, chancery style. In subsequent rolls the membranes are all sewn together at the top, exchequer style. This change, which took place in 1287, has probably no significance other than convenience, as there was a similar change in both the Ipswich and Great Yarmouth borough court rolls from 1289/90.[9] Any kind of agreement may have been open to recognition and enrolment, not just transactions involving property in the city. Other documents were never common, but the first two rolls include an agreement with merchants over tolls, a recognizance of debt, a list of city records to be handed over, and an apprenticeship indenture. The first roll also contains the grant of a messuage in Leicester. Such matters are always rare, but occur occasionally even in the later rolls and an apprentice indenture was enrolled as late as 1405. Most of this non-deed material has already been published in full.[10] Most of the documents enrolled concern property in Norwich and its single suburb. There were, however, even within the city boundaries, areas outside the jurisdiction of the city court. These were the Castle Fee and the fee of the Prior of Norwich, which was centred on the Cathedral (see Fig.). Although there are some deeds enrolled relating to properties in other parts of the city to which the prior was a party, there are none enrolled in these first five rolls relating to property in the two parishes of St Helen or St Mary in the Marsh (which were entirely within the Priory Fee), while the acknowledgement of a deed granting rents from tenements both within and without the Castle Fee was limited to the rent payable from the latter.[11]

As, in practice, enrolment was limited almost entirely to deeds, and to deeds of property in Norwich, so too, in practice, it was only deeds affecting freehold interests that were enrolled. Just one 'lease for years' (creating a leasehold interest) appears on the rolls for 1285-90 and 1306-11 and even this is exceptional as it is a twenty-year lease of a 20s rentcharge and not one of land, which is more usual.[12] This preoccupation with free tenements is still found as late as the early 16th century when, for example, the results of arbitration in a boundary dispute were ordered to be enrolled 'in asmech as they concerne frehold'.[13] This was not unusual. In Ipswich, too, it was deeds concerning free tenements which were enrolled.[14] There was probably a practical reason for this limitation. It is clear from the early 14th-century Norwich

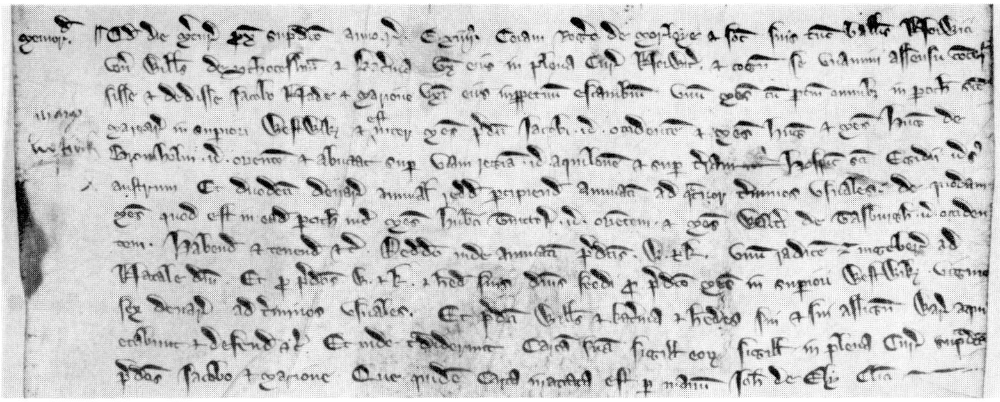

Pl.3a

The enrolled entry of the grant by William de Shotesham and Katerina his wife quoted in translation opposite. It was written by John de Ely and ends with the words inactata est per manum Johannis de Ely clerici 'enrolled by the hand of John de Ely clerk'

Other clerks might end the entries they wrote in different ways e.g.

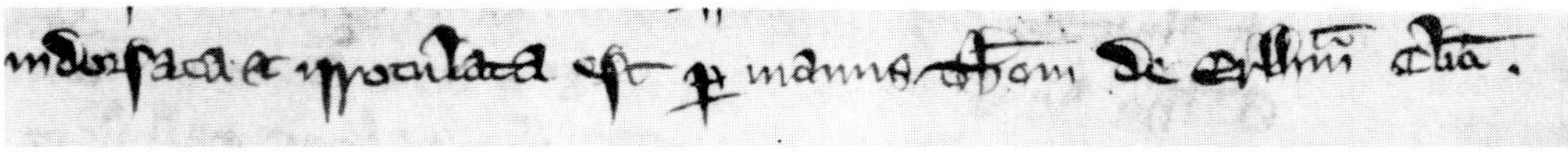

Pl.3b

indorsata et irrotulata est per manus Thome de Erlham clerici
'endorsed and enrolled by the hand of T.de E clerk'

Pl.3c

indorsata est per manum Johannis le Grand clerici
'endorsed by the hand of John le Grand [Graunt] clerk'

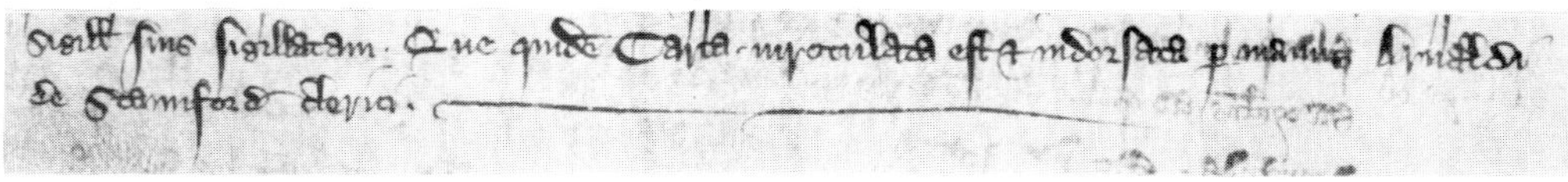

Pl.3d

inrotulata est et indorsata per manus Arnaldi de Staunford clerici
'enrolled and endorsed by the hand of Arnald de Staunford [Stamford] clerk'

custumal that the court rolls would be consulted in cases of dispute.[15] Enrolment would be a more important aid to freeholders in disputes, not only because most freehold interests lasted longer than leasehold interests (with life tenancies an obvious exception) but also because a dispossessed freeholder could recover his house or land in the courts, while a dispossessed leaseholder had only a possible claim for damages.

A typical example of the entries on the rolls is given below. The rolls are written in Latin and so quotations in this paper are generally given in translation:

> Memorandum. That on Wednesday next [before the feast of St Laurence] in the fourteenth year of the reign of Edward [7 August 1286] before Roger de Morleye and his fellows then bailiffs of Norwich came William de Schotesham and Katerina his wife in the full court of Norwich and recognised that they had with unanimous assent granted and given to James Nade and Marion his wife in perpetual exchange one messuage with all appurtenances in the parish of St Margaret in Upper Westwick and it is between a messuage of the foresaid James to the west and a messuage of Hugh de Bromholm to the east and abuts on the king's highway to the north and on land of the hospital of St Giles towards the south. And twelve pence annual rent to be taken yearly at the four usual terms from a certain messuage which is in the same parish between a messuage of Hubert Tinctor to the east and a messuage of Walter de Tasburgh to the west. To have and to hold etc. Paying therefrom yearly to the foresaid William and Katerina one root of ginger at Christmas. And on behalf of the foresaid William and Katerina and their heirs [paying] to the lords of the fee for the foresaid messuage in Upper Westwick twenty-six pence at the usual terms. And the foresaid William and Katerina and their heirs and their assigns warrant acquit and defend etc. And then they handed over (tradiderunt) their deed sealed with their seal in the full court abovesaid to the foresaid James and Marion. Which deed, in truth, was enrolled (inactata) by the hand of John de Ely clerk.[16]

The information given in entries such as this was taken from the original deeds brought by the grantors to the city court (see p.46). Occasionally, this origin is betrayed by the use of a phrase direct from the deed, for example, 'paying to us etc.' instead of 'paying to William and Katerina etc.' - the third person equivalent which could be expected to be used on the rolls. There are other minor differences between a deed and its entry on the rolls. Spelling of proper names, for instance, is as inconsistent here as elsewhere at this date, and can vary considerably between a deed and its entry; and standard phrases were often abbreviated on the rolls. The habendum clause ('to have and to hold'), for example, usually appears in an abbreviated form up to 1290. After 1290 this clause not infrequently runs 'to have and to hold as is witnessed by their deed' (prout carta sua testatur), suggesting that the original deed might include conditions that it was not felt necessary to enrol. Moreover, the lists of witnesses and dating clauses that end original deeds are almost never enrolled. Generally, however, the presence or absence of information on the rolls reflects the contents of the deeds brought to the court. Entries on the early rolls commonly state the rents to be paid out of property granted, including rents reserved to the grantor (as the root of ginger is above, p.45), but this is unusual by 1311. Another rent not mentioned in the above example, but often payable from Norwich tenements, was the landgable, an ancient rent originally payable to the king from certain borough properties. By this date the landgable was collected by the bailiffs, and put towards the fee farm which the city paid annually to the king. The purchase price for the property is rarely mentioned in the rolls, except during the short period 1287-94.

The phrase 'with unanimous assent' (unanimi assensu), used when a conveyance was made by a husband and wife together, was one taken from the original deed. There are no specific references on the rolls to a wife being examined by the court, such as there are on the Ipswich enrolments.[17] Nevertheless, it was clearly necessary for the wife to be present in court and show her consent to the transaction. When William de Pulham enrolled a grant of a messuage in February 1287, and his wife Christiana did not attend the court, the deed was clearly stated to be handed over in her absence; and a grant enrolled by Nicholas Toly in August 1289 was said to have been brought to the court 'in the absence of Alice his wife and without her consent'.[18] There are also several references in the early 14th-century custumal to the wife having to show her consent before the bailiffs in full court.[19]

The final sentence of the entry on the court roll variously describes deeds as being inactata (or inactitata), indorsata or inrotulata. The last two terms give little trouble. Indorsata means 'endorsed', referring to the practice of writing on the back of the original deed to show that it had been produced in court (see p.48) and inrotulata means 'enrolled'. Inactata, on the other hand, is less easily translated, but appears to mean 'enrolled' rather than 'endorsed', as some deeds are described as being inactitata by one clerk and indorsata by another, showing a clear distinction between the two acts.[20] It follows that, where a deed is described as inactitata or inrotulata, the clerk named is the scribe who wrote the entry in the court rolls, though this is not necessarily the case where the entry only mentions endorsement. The two clerks who wrote most of the Norwich court rolls during this period were John de Ely and Thomas de Erlham. John de Ely wrote the early entries and usually ended with inactata. Thomas de Erlham gradually took over in 1289/90 and, once established, normally used indorsata. The entries he wrote are less consistent than those of John de Ely, and at times he left out the initial phrase with the date for several membranes together. Thomas de Erlham was still clerk in 1311, but he was not the only scribe employed after 1290. Two other clerks at least, John le Graunt and Arnald de Staunford, can be clearly identified, either from the wording or from their handwriting.

b) THE PROCESS OF ENROLMENT

Enrolment on the Norwich city court rolls was the final stage in a process, which began with the acknowledgement of a deed before the full court of Norwich. This court sat in the Tolhouse, the precursor of the Guildhall, and was presided over by the four bailiffs who were the chief officers of the city from the early 13th century until the creation of a mayor in 1404.[21] It appears from the dates given on the court rolls that the court could sit for this purpose on any day of the week except Sunday, and it often sat several days running. Both parties to a transfer of property had to come before the court, where the grantor (or seller) acknowledged his grant and handed over his deed to the purchaser. This procedure gave publicity to transfers of land and enabled rival claims to be raised.

During the 13th century, not only were deeds acknowledged before the court, but its officials were often present when they were written. Among the Norwich Private Deeds relating to properties in the parish of St Peter Mancroft (hereafter referred to as City Mancroft deeds[22]), are forty-nine dated between 1250 and 1289. In all but a few of these, the witness lists are headed either by the four bailiffs or by the <u>custos</u> who managed the city when the liberties were in the king's <u>hands.</u> The same is true of all but two of the twenty-two deeds of this date among the records of the Dean and Chapter of Norwich, which relate to properties in the parish of St Peter Mancroft (hereafter called the Dean and Chapter Mancroft deeds[23]). With so many original deeds of this period witnessed by the bailiffs or <u>custos</u>, it is not surprising that some of them also appear to have been written by a clerk in the employ of the city. Before 1290 the lists of witnesses on the original deeds often end with the name of a clerk.[2] Although these clerks are not described as having written the deeds on which they appear, it was traditional for the name of the scribe to be put at the end. A comparison of the handwriting of the deeds shows that those thus ascribed to one clerk were indeed all written by the same man. From these witness lists it appears that Hamon the clerk wrote two of the City Mancroft deeds endorsed in 1260, and Adam one from among the deeds datable to 1270-79. Roger drew up one of the Dean and Chapter and seven of the City Mancroft deeds between 1260 and 1270, while John the clerk was responsible for no fewer than twenty-two of the City Mancroft deeds dated between 1270 and 1289, and for nine of the Dean and Chapter Mancroft deeds of the same period. Of these four clerks, Hamon and Adam were clearly employed by the city, as they also endorsed original deeds to show that they had been acknowledged (see p.48). Hamon is even described in one endorsement as <u>del Tolhus</u> (of the Tolhouse). Roger may well be the same man as the Roger who endorses a deed in 1270, though the endorsement is written in a more flowing hand than the deeds. He may also be the Roger de Hemesby, who is known to have been a city clerk from 1258 to 1276.[25] John cannot be clearly identified in the endorsements, but even if he is not the John de Ely who wrote the early court rolls, he was almost certainly in the employ of the city as he also wrote most of the sixteen agreements concerning stalls in Nedlerowe which were made with the bailiffs in the early 1290s.[26] A deed written by one clerk might be endorsed by another, but this is no argument for the first not being a borough clerk. The references in the court rolls to deeds being enrolled (either <u>inactitata</u> or <u>inrotulata</u>) by one man and endorsed by another show that more than one clerk at a time could be employed on city business.

Soon after 1290 the picture changes. The four bailiffs cease to be personally involved as witnesses to deeds, and merely appear as part of the dating clause in the phrase 'in the time of ... (names) ... bailiffs of Norwich'. At the same time the clerk's name ceases to appear at the end of the witness list, though several of the 1290-99 City Mancroft deeds (apart from the Nedlerowe agreements) were probably still written by John. By 1300-1310, however, the greater number of hands appearing in the deeds suggests that parties were by now using private conveyancers instead of having their deeds written out by borough clerks.[27]

A further element in the acknowledgement before the court was probably the actual conveyance of property granted. A deed could not generally in itself act as a conveyance, and the handing over of property took place by the symbolic gesture of 'livery of seisin'. It was this livery which is likely to have taken place before the bailiffs. From 1288 onwards there occur occasional references in endorsements and enrolments to the payment of 'outpenny' and 'inpenny' to the bailiffs by the grantor and purchaser respectively. The grantor paid 'for leaving his right' (de iure suo exeundo) or 'in sign and testimony of leaving his right' (in signum et testimonium exeundi de iuro suo) and the purchaser 'for entering into his right' (ad ius suum intrando) or 'in sign and testimony of entering as his right' (in signum et testimonium ingrediendi ut ius suum). This payment was in addition to the charges made for endorsement or enrolment which were paid to the clerk. Where a rent was transferred, the role of the court was stated explicitly. A purchaser of a rent only acquired seisin (legal possession) when his right to the rent had been formally acknowledged by the tenant who paid it (attorned). The early 14th-century custumal of Norwich provided that, on the sale of a rent from a tenement not held by the seller, the holder of the tenement should come into court to acknowledge that the rent was payable and so attorn himself to the purchaser,[28] and there is evidence that this practice was not unknown at an earlier date. Following the enrolment of a grant of a 6s rent to John Page in May 1289, for instance, is a note that John son of Clement, the holder of the property, came and gave John Page 2d in the name of seisin and attorned himself to the said John Page.[29] If seisin was being delivered before the court, this would explain the enrolment in March 1311 of letters of attorney to receive as well as to deliver seisin made by both parties to a grant.[30] The more usual, though still uncommon, enrolment of letters of attorney to deliver seisin only might have been explicable on the grounds that they also empowered the attorneys to enrol. Livery of seisin need not always have taken place before the court. The late 13th-century custumals of a number of boroughs, though clearly accepting livery before the borough court as the norm, agree that witness of livery by the neighbourhood was an acceptable substitute.[31]

After this acknowledgement a deed might be endorsed. A typical endorsement (when translated from the Latin) runs:

> Memorandum that this deed (carta) was read in the full court of Norwich and handed over (tradita) by the hands of Walter Gamage of Norwich and Beatrix his wife [the grantors] on Friday in the feast of St Botulph in the sixth year of the reign of King Edward [17 June 1278]. Transacted (acta) by the hand of Adam the clerk.[32]

This form of endorsement (with minor variations) was used from the 1250s to the end of the period under discussion. By no means all late 13th and early 14th-century Norwich deeds, however, were endorsed. The City Mancroft deeds include only two endorsed deeds out of a total of eighteen for 1280-89, only six out of twenty for 1290-99, and seven out of twenty-two for 1300-10. The Dean and Chapter Mancroft deeds had a higher rate of endorsement, but even so only two out of five deeds were endorsed 1285-94 and five out of seven between 1295 and 1310.

These endorsed deeds might also be enrolled, but endorsement did not always imply enrolment. The term acta, (used occasionally at the end of entries) probably meant much the same as indorsata. It obviously did not mean 'enrolled', since the clerk writing the endorsement did not always write the roll entry (see p.46). Moreover, only three of the six City Mancroft deeds which were endorsed 1290-99, were also enrolled, and, of the six Dean and Chapter Mancroft deeds endorsed 1285-99, only two appear on the rolls. The early 14th-century Norwich custumal confirms this by referring to a previous practice of only endorsing and not enrolling married women's deeds.[33] By contrast, all the nine City Mancroft and Dean and Chapter Mancroft deeds endorsed between 1300 and 1310 were also enrolled. This suggests that the practice in endorsing/enrolling deeds at Norwich may have gone through three different stages before 1311. In the earliest period, from the date of the first endorsements on original Norwich Private Deeds in the 1250s, there was probably no provision for enrolment, and deeds could only be endorsed. From the start of enrolment (c. 1285) until soon after 1300, deeds could be endorsed and enrolled, but could also be endorsed without enrolment. Finally, from early in the 14th century, only enrolled deeds seem to be endorsed. In this final stage, documents may not have been endorsed until after their enrolment. This would explain the entries on Roll 5 (1307-11), which end with 'endorsed by the hand' (indorsata per manus), without giving the name of the clerk, as if the scribe was unsure which clerk was to write the endorsement. In exceptional circumstances, a deed might be enrolled but not endorsed. For example, when Simon, son of Seman Wrinel, was held to be under age, his grant of a stall was not endorsed, though it was enrolled as usual.[34] At Winchester, borough deeds were sealed with the common seal, but there is no sign of this happening at Norwich.[35]

The early Norwich court rolls contain no evidence that such enrolment was restricted to citizens, and throughout them there are many examples where neither party to a deed is described as such. This is not conclusive, as personal descriptions are by no means consistent, but, had much emphasis been laid on citizenship, it is likely that it would always have been mentioned. Nor was there any restriction to enrolment on the grounds of sex, with many recognitions being made by single women or widows, or by married women together with their husbands. It was necessary, however, for a grantor to be of full age, and in several cases this was queried. In February 1310 the age of majority in Norwich was stated to be sixteen; and although a quitclaim by the children of the former rector of Carlton Forehoe, had been enrolled in February 1287 without question when the son, William, was only fifteen, this may have been because, his sister, Matilda, was of full age.[36] The cost of enrolment was comparatively low. The Norwich custumal from the early 14th-century Book of Customs mentions payment to the clerk of only 2d for endorsement and 4d for enrolment.[37] Even with the addition of the inpenny and outpenny paid to the bailiffs, the total was no more than 8d. At London, by contrast, 2s was being paid to the alderman for livery of seisin alone as early as the 12th century, and throughout the Ipswich recognizance rolls of 1294-1327 there are frequent references to the payment of 2s to the bailiffs for the recognizance (acknowledgement), and a further 6d or 12d (according to whether the grantee was a burgess) for seisin.[38]

Enrolment did not prevent a deed from being challenged subsequently, and there are several examples in the rolls of rival claims which were often made by the widow of the testator or grantor. It is not clear whether there was a time limit on claims, such as the year and a day often imposed elsewhere, as most of the challenges are undated. The longest lapse of time noted was when a deed was disputed a little over a year after its enrolment.[39]

As the dating clause of deeds was not usually included in the entry, the only date we have for most enrolled deeds is that of their acknowledgement. This is the same date as appears on the endorsements. Although the enrolments themselves are not dated, it seems likely that deeds were enrolled straight after their production in court. Documents are entered on the rolls in strict chronological order (of acknowledgement), which, with up to six entries a week, could hardly have been achieved had there been any regular delay between appearance in court and enrolment. In the two periods considered in detail, such few lapses from chronological order as occur can mostly be explained by the misplacing of a membrane or the later filling up of a gap.[40]

Although there seems to have been no delay between acknowledgement and enrolment, there is sometimes evidence of delay between the writing of an original deed and its being produced in court. There are, for instance, many examples of the same person being a party to consecutive entries on the rolls, the sequence not being attributable to an exchange of properties, where it looks as though several transactions may have been kept back, so that all could be enrolled at the same time. Generally, however, the delay was not very great. Of twenty-one original Norwich deeds, dated 1281-1311,[41] ten were endorsed either on the same day on which they were written or within a week. Another five were endorsed within the month, and in only one case was the delay longer than six months. This was where a grant by William de Burtoft and Ysabella his wife, dated 18 May 1284, was not endorsed until June 1292.[42] Delayed enrolment must always have been limited by the fact that the acknowledgement which constituted the first stage of the process had to be made by the grantor. This meant that no deed could normally be enrolled after the grantor's death. Where a delay amounted to several years there is no reason to assume that acknowledgement before the court and livery of seisin could not have taken place some time before enrolment. In another example of long delay, discussed by Hudson and Tingey, John Page initiated the enrolment on 7 February 1289 of two quitclaims made to him in 1278 and 1282.[43] Both these quitclaims had been acknowledged and endorsed at the time they were made but not enrolled. This enrolment required special permission from the court, probably not because of the date of the documents, but because acknowledgement was usually made by the grantor, while in this case enrolment was sought by the grantee. In such cases a deed would presumably have to be re-acknowledged before the court before enrolment. Where the delay was shorter, however, there need have been no acknowledgement or livery of seisin prior to the date of enrolment. A delay of several months would seem more likely to occur where a private rather than a borough clerk was employed to write the original deed, but too few 13th-century deeds are both dated and endorsed to establish this.

c) TYPES OF TRANSACTION

The main forms of document enrolled on the Norwich court rolls are grants, quitclaims, demises for life or at fee farm and wills.

i) *Grants*

By far the greater number of enrolments were grants. These made up

73% of all deeds enrolled in 1285-90, rising to 79% of enrolments in 1306-11. In a grant, property was 'granted and given' (dedisse et concessisse) to the purchaser, and grants were used to transfer land or rents. The form was the same whether the purpose of transfer was a sale, a gift, a reallocation of property within the family, or a mortgage. A high proportion of these grants (77% in 1285-90 and 89.5% in 1306-11) conveyed houses or land (tenements) in Norwich and its suburb, the remainder conveying rents. A few grants, like the example given on p.45, transferred both rents and tenements (5.5 and 2% respectively). Sometimes there is a clear connection between the tenement and the rent conveyed. In July 1311, for example, Peter de Scothouwe and Agatha, his wife, enrolled a grant transferring to William Bateman a shop in the Spicery, together with a 3s rent from a shop to the east.[44] Here, perhaps, both shops had once been owned by Peter and Agatha, who had sold the shop to the east to a third party, reserving a rent of 3s. Now they were selling the remaining shop, together with the reserved rent, to William Bateman. However, there need have been no connection between the two interests granted. By a grant enrolled in February 1287, for instance, John de Cantelof and Catherine, his wife, transferred to James Nade a messuage in the parish of St Margaret Westwyk together with a rent of 2s 6d payable from a messuage some distance away in the parish of St Stephen.[45] The numbers of grants of both tenements and rents together are small, no more than twenty-six for both periods altogether.

The majority of the grants of tenements enrolled seem to have been straightforward sales rather than rearrangements of family property. Several grants in frankmarriage (maritagium, a gift on marriage to a son or daughter) are recorded, but there are only twenty-four of these and other grants to named or possible relations among all grants enrolled in 1285-90 and 1306-11; and two of these were clearly not gifts, as the grantees paid in one case 100s and in the other 6 marks. A common way of reallocating family interests at this date was by grant to a third party followed by a regrant, but there is only one clear example of this during these two periods. By deeds enrolled in November 1287, Matilda, the daughter of William de Welles, granted to Thomas, vicar of Ringland, on her remarriage, various rents and tenements in Norwich. These were immediately regranted to Matilda and her new husband.[46] The only unexpected feature of this transaction is that a purchase price of 20 marks was paid for the grant and 24 marks for the regrant. In another grant and regrant, Roger Benjamin and Edith, his wife, granted a messuage to Ralph Boleman by a deed enrolled in February 1287. By the following entry, the same messuage was granted back to Roger alone by Ralph and Margaret, his wife.[47] The purpose of this transaction is not clear. Edith could have been joined in the same grant, as Margaret presumably was in the regrant, simply to defeat her right to dower (see p.55). The emphasis in the entries, however, on Edith having formerly been the wife of John de Hahill, makes it probable that the intention here was to destroy an interest she had acquired from her late husband. It would be wrong to infer that family arrangements as to land hardly existed in Norwich. It is merely that they play a very small part in the enrolled deeds.

The other grants enrolled conveyed rents. In contrast to the grants of tenements enrolled, the proportion of grants conveying rents fell between 1285-90 and 1306-11 from 28.5 to 12.5%. Grants could be used to transfer rents, which had either originated as rents reserved to the seller on a sale of property (service rents), or as rents charged (rentcharges) by the holder on the property in favour of someone else. The deeds enrolled do not always give the amount of rent transferred. Judging from the 130 grants that mention specific amounts, however, the value of rents granted by a single deed changed little between 1285-90 and 1306-11. Almost half (47%) of these 130 grants conveyed rents totalling 1s to 5s; rents worth from 5s to 10s formed another third (34.5%). From the very few grants of rents totalling less than 1s a year, it seems that it was considered hardly worth enrolling grants if they transferred only such low rents. Of the six rents worth under 1s a year whose grants are enrolled, four were not the subject of grants on their own, but were coupled with tenements in the same grant. This is not to say, however, that rents worth less than 1s a year were not considered worth conveying. On the contrary, the amount transferred by any single grant was often the sum of several low rents. When, for instance, in July 1289 Semannus Grym enrolled the grant to his son Henry of 3s 7d worth of rents, this was made up of no fewer than four separate 2d rents from different properties, one of 6d, one of 12d, one of 17d and a clove rent for good measure.[48]

ii) *Quitclaims*

Quitclaims made up 25% of all deeds enrolled in 1285-90, and decreased to 16.5% of all enrolments in 1306-11. By a quitclaim, limited interests in tenements or rents were 'given and quitclaimed' (dedisse et quietumclamasse i.e. released) to the holder. Occasionally, the same entry in the rolls includes both a grant of one property and the quitclaim of an interest in another. Sometimes the connection between the grant and the quitclaim is fairly clear. In December 1308, for instance, John de Stonhus and Isabella, his wife, enrolled the grant of a messuage to William But together with the quitclaim of a 2d rent from an adjoining messuage to the north.[49] Probably John and Isabella originally owned at least part of both messuages, but had decided to split the property, and sold the northern half to William But, reserving a rent of 2d a year. Now William But was buying the southern half as well and, at the same time, had persuaded John and Isabella to extinguish the 2d rent he was paying for the northern messuage. There need not always be this clear relationship between the two transactions. There is none, for instance, between a quitclaim by Thomas de Cauz releasing his rights in a 1s 2d rent to Geoffrey le Goos, and the accompanying grant of the advowson of St Margaret's church, which were enrolled together in August 1287.[50] Such joint entries, however, were rare and there are no more than half a dozen altogether in the two five-year periods looked at in detail. Although the numbers of joint grant and quitclaim entries and of grants of both tenements and rents are small, the situation which often gave rise to them was probably a common one. That the same person should hold one messuage and be in receipt of a rent from a messuage next door could be the natural consequence of sub-division of tenements by subinfeudation before 1290.

The nature of the rights released by quitclaims varied considerably. Rights to rents were quitclaimed as well as rights to tenements, and thirteen of the quitclaims enrolled 1285-90 and nineteen of those enrolled 1306-11 were solely or in part concerned with rents. No reason is given for a significant percentage of the quitclaims enrolled,[51] but the remainder were used for a number of different purposes. There are quitclaims, for instance, by widows, some, but not necessarily all, releasing rights of dower. A few others are by the losing parties to court actions, and there is one by a joint tenant. Executors often used a form of quitclaim with the word 'sell' (vendidisse) added when selling property in accordance with the terms of a will. There are also a few quitclaims made by the tenant in demesne, the holder of the property, back to his lord (i.e. back to a former owner or son or wife of a former owner), and, between 1285 and 1290, five quitclaims by sisters or brothers of the purchaser were enrolled. The situation is not clear, but a couple of references to division between children suggest that Norwich, like Ipswich, may have had partible inheritance (i.e. real property was shared equally between sons or between sons and daughters).[52] Finally, there are quitclaims by sons or daughters of former owners. This was probably a sensible precaution in the case of property left by will, as the custumal mentions the problem of intruders into devised tenements.[53] The rights being released in some of these quitclaims, however, as in some of those made by widows and some of those about which no information is given, are probably the rights of lordship, automatically retained by a grantor on a conveyance by subinfeudation. Any rents reserved on such a conveyance would also be extinguished. This use would explain the inclusion in so many of the quitclaims enrolled in the early rolls of habendum (to have and to hold) and reddendo (paying) clauses. In later law such clauses were not considered necessary in a release, but in terms of the complicated tenurial relationships likely to have been created by frequent subinfeudation, it was important to say of whom the property was now to be held and which rents were still to be paid. Conspicuous by their almost complete absence are the quitclaims made as extra security by grantors, which were so common in the later medieval period.[54] There are, however, a few combined grant/quitclaim entries on the rolls where property is granted, given and quitclaimed (concessisse, dedisse et quietumclamasse).[55]

iii) *Demises for life and at fee farm*

A very small proportion of the deeds enrolled (1.5% in 1285-90, and 2% in 1306-11) were demises for life or at fee farm. In a demise, or lease, for life, property was let for the lifetime of a person, usually the lessee, and reverted to the lessor after their death. This could be done either to acquire an income from the rent reserved, or to provide for a member of the family. Both uses appear in the rolls. Rents were reserved on two of the total of seven demises for life enrolled during these two periods, while another three clearly represent a family arrangement, with the daughter of the lessor being one of the lessees.

The ten demises or leases at fee farm on the other hand, were exclusively financial in nature. (The words used were 'granted and demised at fee farm', concessisse et dimississe ad feodi firmam.) A demise at fee farm (like a grant) passed an inheritable and transferable interest, and this form of conveyance seems to have been used when the seller wished to retain greater control than usual over the property. In most of the demises at fee farm (as also in one of the demises for life reserving a high rent), the seller sought to protect his rent by clauses requiring the purchaser to maintain the property in good order at his own cost, and giving a right to re-enter if the rent was unpaid or the property not kept in good repair. The rents reserved on four of the demises at fee farm were further protected by recognizances (acknowledgements in court) made by the purchasers of their obligation to pay. As has already been mentioned (see p.43) only one lease for years was enrolled during these two periods.

iv) *Wills*

Wills never made up more than a very small percentage of all deeds enrolled, (0.5% in 1285-90 and 2.5% in 1306-11) and their enrolment was never a matter of course. Norwich, however, followed many other boroughs in allowing property within the city to be left by will. Only wills devising tenements or rents in Norwich were enrolled, and then the enrolment was usually limited to the clause containing the devise, followed by a note of probate. According to the early 14th-century custumal, Norwich also followed other boroughs in allowing only tenements purchased by the testator to be devised, and not those he had acquired by inheritance. Women could leave property held by them before marriage, subject to their husbands' right to hold the property for life (right to curtesy), and several chapters of the custumal deal with a devise in tail (limited to the issue of the devisee) and the possibility of property being sold to pious uses if a devisee died without issue.[56] In such circumstances property could be sold for the benefit of a testator's soul many years after his death. Even this limited enrolment of wills, however, did not always take place. Mary Bateson describes a Norwich case of 1311 quoted in the London Liber Ordinacionum, in which a will was disputed on the grounds that it had not been enrolled or recited before the bailiffs and seisin had not been delivered by the bailiffs as custom demanded.[57] The jurors found against the custom, and reported that about sixteen years before, an ordinance had been made requiring executors to prove and enrol wills but there had never been any compulsion. Certainly the city private deeds contain at least one will for the period 1306-11 which devises property in Norwich but is neither endorsed nor enrolled.[58]

It is also noticeable that the wills enrolled were those including direct devises of property, generally to the testator's immediate family, rather than wills that only left property to be sold. Sales and quitclaims by the executors of twenty-one men whose wills left property to be sold were enrolled both at the beginning and end of the period, but only three of their wills were also enrolled.

d) REASONS FOR ENROLMENT

Basically, enrolment constituted a safeguard against the three perils of fire, forgery and theft. Dealers in property on a large scale might be expected to make special use of enrolment to protect their financial interests, and the activities of only five people would account for between a quarter and a third of the entries on the first roll.[59] A man owning a single messuage on the other hand, might consider his position was safeguarded sufficiently by the publicity surrounding acknowledgement before the court, and be deterred by the cost of enrolment. The Norwich custumal, however, suggests more specific reasons. Enrolment is mentioned in the custumal in connection with the three types of transaction. The first two involved married women. At Common Law a married woman could convey neither the property she held before marriage nor any that she had since acquired jointly with her husband. The property could be conveyed by her husband, but even if his wife were joined in the deed, such a conveyance could always be upset after her husband's death on the grounds that her consent was forced. According to the custumal, however, endorsement and enrolment in the city court created a conveyance by a married woman that could not be upset later. The custumal refers to a previous practice of only endorsing, and not enrolling, such deeds, and requires that in future they should be both endorsed and enrolled.[60] Secondly, enrolment could play a part in defeating a wife's right to dower. This was the right of a wife to a life interest in a proportion, not only of that property that her husband held at his death, but of all property of which he had ever been seised during the marriage. The confusion this could cause in a busy property market may easily be imagined, and is nicely illustrated by the case of Margaret, the widow of Gervase de Irstede, who claimed dower in October 1289 out of a property which had changed hands three times since it was owned by her husband.[61] A woman could not release her rights to dower during the lifetime of her husband but, according to the custumal, if she were joined in a conveyance with her husband and the deed was enrolled, this would bar any future claim.[62] The extent of a wife's right to dower in Norwich is not known, but it is probable that the city followed London in giving a widow dower in a third part of her husband's property. In these regulations, Norwich displayed a more favourable attitude towards married women than was shown by many other towns. In Bury St Edmunds, for instance, a husband needed no consent either to sell his wife's lands or to sell his own so as to bar her right to dower, and the same was true at Nottingham. At Lincoln, a wife's consent was not needed to bar dower, and at Godmanchester a husband could sell lands acquired jointly with his wife without her consent and against her will.[63] The problem faced by boroughs was how to enable urban property to be freely transferred, and to avoid confusion, while ensuring that married women were not fraudulently deprived of their property rights by deeds to which they did not fully consent. The compromise described in the Norwich custumal required that, where a married woman joined in a conveyance of property held with her husband, she was to be examined by the bailiffs to prove that her consent was genuine, and the deed was to be enrolled as well as endorsed as a permanent record.[64] Where a wife was joined in a conveyance to defeat any future right to dower, the need for both husband and wife to acknowledge the deed in open court and to enrol it was probably sufficient to deter fraudulent grants.

Thirdly, the custumal mentions enrolment in connection with wills. It provided that, once they had been proved by the ecclesiastical authorities in the usual way, any testaments devising tenements in Norwich should be proved before the bailiffs. The whole clause mentioning the devise was to be enrolled and the will endorsed.[65]

e) THE EFFECT OF THE CUSTUMAL

The number of deeds enrolled rose from 413 during 1285-90 to 535 in 1306-11. Such an increase might be expected in an expanding city, especially since jurisdiction over the leet of Newgate (Surrey Street), which formerly belonged to Norwich Priory, had been granted to the citizens in 1305.[66] The explanation, however, may not be so simple. In the first place, there is a noticeable drop in the number of deeds enrolled for the years between these two periods, as is shown in the following table:

July 1285	-	May 1290	413
August 1291	-	July 1296	291
October 1296	-	September 1301	272
October 1301	-	September 1306	389
October 1306	-	October 1311	535

Any argument based on this drop in enrolments assumes, of course, that these intervening rolls are complete. It is never possible to be sure at any time, when the change from one month to the next occurs at the end of a membrane, that an intermediate membrane has not been lost, though the general chronological order of the rolls should make it possible to pick up any lengthy gaps. Unfortunately, during the sixteen years 1290-1306, there are four periods of between six and thirteen months each during which the individual entries on the rolls were not dated. The total number of deeds enrolled during these years, however, is not significantly different from the numbers enrolled in preceeding and succeeding years for whose entries dates are given. In fact, the year during which the fewest deeds were enrolled (1296, twenty-seven entries) is also one whose entries are all dated, and where the changes from one membrane to the next both occur in the middle of a month.[67] It therefore looks as if there was a genuine drop in the numbers of documents enrolled between 1290 and 1306. If enrolment only began in 1285, the 1285-90 figures may be increased by retrospective enrolments but there is no evidence of this.

Secondly, there is an apparent change in the nature of the transactions being enrolled, as set out below:

	1285-1290	1306-1311
Grants	300 (73%)	423 (79%)
Quitclaims	104 (25%)	88 (16.5%)
Demises for life or at fee farm	7 (1.5%)	10 (2%)
Wills	2 (0.5%)	14 (2.5%)

To some extent the reduction in the number of quitclaims may be a result of _Quia Emptores_. Before 1290 the seller of property usually became the feudal lord of the purchaser, but in 1290 this practice was abolished by the statute of _Quia Emptores_. As the object of many quitclaims of this date was to eliminate rights of lordship, one might expect this abolition of subinfeudation to lead to a decrease in the number of quitclaims made.

The deeds enrolled, however, can be looked at in another way, and that is to consider the increase in the enrolment of the three types of transaction mentioned by the custumal. The proportion of wills enrolled was always small, and it is clear that not even those devising Norwich property were necessarily being enrolled (see p.54). Nevertheless, there is a considerable rise in the number appearing on the rolls between 1285 and 1311. Only two probates of wills are enrolled between 1285 and 1290, and only another thirteen between 1290 and 1306, but as many as fourteen were proved and enrolled during the five years 1306-11.

Far more substantial is the growth in the enrolment of the other two categories mentioned in the custumal, namely transfers of married women's property, and deeds to which wives were joined to defeat their right of dower. These need to be taken together, as both will appear in the rolls as conveyances made jointly by husbands and wives. (Even a grant of property held by a wife before marriage would appear as a joint grant, because a husband acquired a life interest in his wife's real estate on marriage.) The number of joint (husband and wife) grants enrolled rose from 173 (58% of grants or 42% of all deeds enrolled) in 1285-90 to 358 (86% and 67% respectively) in 1306-11. The number of joint quitclaims (where the same consideration sometimes applied) rose from forty-one (40% of all quitclaims or 10% of all enrolled deeds) to fifty (55% and 10.5% respectively), although the total of quitclaims enrolled dropped between these two periods. In fact, the increase in the number of joint grants alone (185) is greater than the difference between the number of deeds enrolled in 1306-11 (535) and those enrolled in either 1285-90 (413, difference 122) or 1301-06 (389, difference 146). Though the numbers concerned are too small to be conclusive, some support for the suggestion that the 1306-11 rolls show a disproportionate rise in the number of joint conveyances comes from the City Mancroft deeds. Of ten joint deeds dated 1285-99, only two were enrolled, as opposed to four out of five enrolled in 1300-10. At the same time, the proportion of deeds by men alone, which were enrolled, remained almost constant, with two out of ten enrolled 1285-99, and two out of nine 1300-10.[68]

When these joint conveyances and wills are added together, the proportion of the rolls taken up by transactions mentioned by the custumal rises from 52.5% in 1285-90 to 80.5% in 1306-11. How far this rise can be attributed to the Norwich custumal depends in part on whether the increased number of husband and wife joint grants was the result of a change in the pattern of property holding. Is it just the result of women in Norwich having acquired more interests in property, either jointly with their husbands, or independently before their marriage? This seems unlikely to be the case. The rise in the proportion of deeds made to husbands and wives between 1285 and 1311 is very small: 26% of all conveyances enrolled (105) to 28% (145). Furthermore, the proportion of joint grants in which it appears likely that the wife had acquired an interest in the property before marriage actually fell from 10% (17) to 7½% (26).[69] As the numbers of grants made to husbands and wives, and of grants where the property conveyed may be held by the right of the wife are so low, it is likely that, in at least half the joint grants enrolled, the wife had no present interest in the property granted, and was joined in the deed only to bar any future right to dower. This is the more probable as it is common practice throughout the rolls for grants to be made by husbands and wives jointly but to husbands alone. Even when a grant was made to a husband and wife together, the property was often limited to the heirs and assigns of the husband alone, so that the wife acquired only a life interest.

A further problem in attributing the rise in enrolment to the custumal stems from the fact that we do not know exactly when this was written. The earliest copy survives in the Book of Customs, which Hudson and Tingey date between 1306 and 1311.[70] Though it is clear that one requirement of the custumal, namely the need for a wife to show her consent to a joint conveyance, was taken seriously between 1285 and 1290, the quotation by Mary Bateson from the London Liber Ordinacionum suggests that the regulations concerning wills were made not earlier than 1295.[71] When, between 1295 and 1306, such regulations were put in the codified form known as 'the custumal' must remain in doubt. However, the increase in the rolls after 1306, in precisely those types of document required by the custumal to be enrolled, suggests that this took place either shortly before, or at the time, the Book of Customs was compiled.

f) CONCLUSIONS ON ENROLMENT

It is no new suggestion that the privilege which Norwich shared with other boroughs, of enabling the property of married women to be conveyed and their rights to dower to be defeated, by the enrolment of deeds in the borough court, was a great inducement to enrol.[72] In spite of its advantages, however, the inhabitants of few towns took up enrolment as enthusiastically as those of Norwich. It must always have been necessary to balance the benefits arising against the cost, and the low cost of enrolment at Norwich at this date may well have been a factor in encouraging the large numbers of deeds enrolled there in the late 13th and early 14th centuries. More surprising is the apparent change in the use made of the early court rolls during this short period of twenty-six years. From 1285 to 1290 they seem to be used as a general register of deeds. By 1306-11 their function is more specialised, with 80.5% of all deeds enrolled having married women as co-grantors. Also of interest is the reduction in the number of deeds enrolled between 1290 and 1306, and the suggested revitalisation of enrolment by the early 14th-century custumal. It is impossible to tell whether the drop in the number of enrolments was accompanied by a corresponding drop in the number of documents acknowledged before the court. In part, however, it may have been a drop in the number of acknowledgements that led to reduced enrolment between 1290 and 1306. Before 1290 it may have been a common occurrence for the parties to a conveyance to come to the city court, to have their agreement witnessed by the bailiffs, and employ a borough clerk to draw up a deed. The clerk would have had both the opportunity and the interest to encourage the parties to acknowledge the deed before the next court. The deed could then have been enrolled or not according to the wishes of the parties. After 1290, however, deeds were rarely witnessed by the bailiffs, and probably were more often drawn up away from the court. In such circumstances the inducement required to persuade a grantor to acknowledge and/or enrol his deed would be the greater. Deeds conveying married women's property were probably always acknowledged, but the custumal would have provided further inducement by requiring attornment before the court on the transfer of existing rents (see p.48), as well as by its provisions concerning dower. It is interesting to note that, while the custumal appears to have had the effect of increasing enrolment, any financial advantage from this was gained by the clerks rather than the city. Only outpenny and inpenny were paid to the bailiffs, and these were not dependent on enrolment, while the charges for endorsement and enrolment were paid to the clerks.

2. PROPERTY AND PROPERTY INTERESTS

a) CHANGES BETWEEN THE 1280s AND 1306-11

The principal difference between the deeds enrolled 1285-90 and those enrolled 1306-11 lies in the change in terminology caused by the statute of *Quia Emptores* in 1290. Before 1290 the usual method of transferring property was by subinfeudation, whereby the purchaser became the feudal tenant of the grantor to whom he would then pay a rentservice as his feudal lord, for example, the payment of a root of ginger by James Nade and Marion to William de Schotesham and Katerina referred to on p.45. In an original deed the *habendum* clause (to have and to hold) would normally run 'to have and to hold from me [the grantor] and my heirs'. This clause is rarely given in full in the enrolments, but it can be assumed from the 160 rent-services reserved on grants and demises enrolled 1285-90, that it was normal for transfers in Norwich before 1290 to be by subinfeudation. The statute of *Quia Emptores* (1290) abolished subinfeudation, and thereafter the purchaser of property became the feudal tenant of the grantor's lord. This is reflected in original deeds by a change in the *habendum* clause to 'to have and to hold of the chief lord(s) of the fee', and by rentservices no longer being reserved; and most enrolments of grants made 1306-11 include an *habendum* clause in this form. On the other hand, there are still nineteen examples of property being granted to be held of the grantor. A few of these deeds may have been drawn up before 1290, and two others are grants limited to the issue of the grantees (in tail) which, like leases for life, were not covered by the statute. The majority, however, are probably just examples of outdated conveyancing.

The economic effect of *Quia Emptores*, on the other hand, appears to have been very small. Of the 153 rentservices reserved on grants between 1285 and 1290, 84% (126) were of 1d or less, the majority being clove rents. In most of the transactions enrolled, the grantor clearly expected to be repaid by a lump sum rather than by a reserved rent. Of the remainder, fewer than ten grants reserved rents worth over 5s to 10s (5.5%), and only two reserved rents of over 10s. In spite of *Quia Emptores*, it is surprising to find that forty rents were still reserved to the grantor between 1306 and 1311. Again a high proportion (though a far smaller number than in 1285-90) were nominal rents of 1d and under (62½%, 26). Only one rent worth between 5s and 10s was reserved, but the number of rents worth over 10s doubled to four. The most unusual of these rents was an annuity of 10 marks payable to Nicholas de Plumpstede and Sibill, his wife, for their lives, in return for a grant of all their messuages, buildings, goods and chattels.[73] An interesting point is that fewer than half these rents were reserved from properties to be held from the grantor (i.e. subinfeudated). The *habendum* clause is not always given, but many of the rents are payable from properties expressed as being held from the chief lord of the fee. Apparently it was not yet felt that the abolition of subinfeudation had also abolished a grantor's right to reserve a rent, though later an express grant of a rentcharge in favour of the grantor would be thought necessary to achieve the same result, and there is one example of this on the later rolls. Some higher rents, however, were already being reserved in 1285-90, not on grants, but on demises for life or at fee farm, which usually protected the lessor's investment, either by limiting the demise (for life), or by giving the lessor a right of re-entry if the property was not adequately maintained.[74] Theoretically, demises at fee farm should have been abolished in 1290 but, for a time at least, they may have been thought conditional on the maintenance of the property conveyed and so not covered by the statute.[75]

b) HOW THE PROPERTYHOLDERS OBTAINED THEIR INCOME

There are two possible explanations for the large number of nominal rents reserved during 1285-90. The first is that it had become customary, on a sale of property, to take the purchase price as a lump sum rather than in the form of a reserved rent. The second explanation is that economic rents were still being reserved on sales of property (i.e. the higher rents reserved 1285-90), but that the large number of nominal rents reflect a move on the part of landholders looking for income away from rents reserved on grants (assize rents), to rents payable by tenants for years or at will. As already mentioned, (see p.43), only documents transferring freehold interests were normally enrolled, and only one lease for years appears on the rolls 1285-90 and 1306-11. Apart from this enrolment, there is only one reference to a lease for years in these rolls.[76] Tenancies at will, by their nature, were not created by a formal document which could be enrolled. Without, therefore, far more work on Norwich documents of this date, it is impossible to say to what extent Norwich tenements were occupied by tenants for years or at will. There is some evidence, however, to suggest that property owners were still looking to freehold rather than to leasehold rents for their income. Freehold rents might be reserved on grants or demises for life or at fee farm, as opposed to rents payable under a lease for years or by tenants at will. Of these freehold rents, those reserved on grants or demises at fee farm, might be termed perpetual because, unlike rents paid by lessees for life, they were theoretically payable for ever. One owner of property in Norwich was the city. In the twenty-first year of the reign of Edward 1 (1292/3) Peter Flynt, the city chamberlain, accounted for 63s received from rents of the town of Norwich. No more rents are mentioned until the roll starts again after a gap of several years in 1300/01 (29 Edward 1). In that year Peter Flynt accounted, under the heading of rents, for 44s 8d received in assize rents, 40s received from Nedlerowe, and 40s from the woad market. He also received a total of 22d from three named individuals. The receipts under this heading remain the same up to 32 Edward 1 (1303/4), in which year he also accounts separately for 9s 6d received for the hire (conductio) of houses. No rents are given after 32 Edward 1.[77] It is not clear how the rent of 63s received in 1292/3 was made up, but the situation is clearer in 1300/01-1303/4. The 44s 8d received is declared to be from rents of assize (i.e. reserved rents), and the 40s for the woad market is paid under an agreement with the woad merchants of Amiens and Corbie made on 29 June 1286.[78] The 40s received from Nedlerowe is explained by the City Mancroft deeds, 1290-99.[79] These include no fewer than sixteen undertakings to pay the bailiffs annually, in perpetuity, 2s for each stall which the bailiffs had allowed to be built in Nedlerowe. Even assuming that the 22d received comes from tenants for years or at will as well as the 9s 6d paid for hire, the bulk of the income that the city chamberlain received from rents clearly came from freehold rents. The relationship between the income accounted for by the chamberlain and that received by the bailiffs at this date is not entirely clear, but the bailiffs' income appears to have consisted basically of the landgable rent, market tolls and profits of court.[80] They may also have received the assize rents when necessary. It is most unlikely that they had a separate source of income in non-freehold rents, and it is clear from the court rolls and the City Mancroft deeds that they were currently extending their/the chamberlain's income from perpetual rents and charges. Apart from the Nedlerowe payments already mentioned, several late 13th-century licences to encroach on lanes, the market place, and the river bank are enrolled, all increasing the licensee's perpetual liability to landgable. The amounts of money involved here were small, the largest increase being paid by Master Alan de Frestone, who had built a quay on the east end of his messuage, and whose liability for landgable was raised from 5d to 17d.[81] On the other hand, William Harding, by an agreement of 1 July 1310, extended the right of the bailiffs of Norwich to distrain on his property to secure an annual rent of as much as 40s, which he owed for a stall which they had demised to him in fee.[82]

The great Norwich rival to the city establishment was the Priory of the Holy Trinity. Although most of the Priory officials received some rents from Norwich properties, only two, the cellarer and the almoner, received a substantial part of their income from this source.[83] Unfortunately, neither the relevant rent rolls of the cellarer, nor the account or rent rolls of the almoner, specify the nature of the Norwich rents paid.[84] The cellarer's rent rolls for 1298 and 1319 suggest that the rents paid were assize rents, both by such comments as 'for his houses' and 'from the house devised to him and his father', and because the amounts paid are low, rarely over 2s for the quarter and often under 1s.[85] The rents on the earliest almoner's rent roll, for 1336/7, are similarly low with only two out of eighty-nine Norwich rents being of 2s or over for the quarter. The likelihood that these are assize rents is strengthened by the fact that the same person sometimes paid for more than one property, and by the considerable amounts of arrears due. John de Carletone, for instance, who should have paid 12d twice a year for property in the parish of St Stephen, owed 6s, and John Bumstede, who should have paid two rents of 3s twice a year for two properties in the parish of St Peter Mancroft, owed the grand total of £4 4s.[86] Not all the Priory rents were perpetual. The court rolls for 1291 include two demises for lives made by the prior, and there is another of a shop dated September 1299 among the Dean and Chapter Mancroft deeds.[87] This may indicate a move on the part of the Priory towards leases for lives (still freehold interests). At the same time the Priory was increasing its holding of perpetual rents, as is shown by a demise at fee farm made by the prior to Roger de Tudenham and enrolled in December 1298.[88] The continued importance of perpetual rents as a source of income is also illustrated by four of the six demises at fee farm enrolled between 1285 and 1290. Of these, one was granted by the warden of St Mary Magdalene Hospital, another by the abbot of Woburn, and the other two by John Clerk, son of Adam Page, who plays a large part in the early enrolled deeds.[89] These are the very people, the heads of religious institutions and a man with considerable property interests in Norwich, who one might expect to have changed from freehold rents to leasing for years or at will, had there been such a trend in Norwich at this date.[90] The move towards purely nominal reserved rents before 1290, therefore, was probably dictated by other factors. Whether it was more convenient to pay for a purchase by a reserved rent, or the payment of a lump sum would depend, for instance, on the amount of cash available in the city and the ease with which such a lump sum could be raised.

c) THE VALUE OF PROPERTY

If freehold rents were being used for investment in Norwich at this date, it might be wondered why the sums reserved, even when nominal payments of 1d and below are excluded, are so low. That some Norwich properties could have a higher annual value than the reserved rents suggest, is indicated by the prices paid for rents and tenements between October 1285 and May 1290. During this period prices paid for grants of both rents and tenements are commonly entered in the rolls. Altogether, the prices are given for 15 grants of rent. One is a mortgage where the amount of money advanced (26s 8d) bears little relation to the value of the rent (40s a year), but the remaining fourteen rents were sold, on average, for a little under ten times their annual value. For the same period, we have the prices paid for seventy-three grants of tenements. Assuming that these were also valued at roughly ten times their yearly rental, eight (11%) of these payments would represent annual rents of 30s and over. The three highest prices paid are one of 50 marks (£33 6s 8d), and two of 40 marks (£26 13s 4d), suggesting possible annual values of 66s 8d and 53s 4d respectively. These are much higher than either the rents reserved or the rents conveyed would lead us to expect. On the other hand, using the same reckoning, thirty-three (45%) of the prices paid represent annual values of under 5s. This need not surprise us. Neither the lump sum paid nor the rent reserved need reflect the total value of a tenement. Apart from the obvious point that a purchaser might pay for property partly by a lump sum and partly by a reserved rent, both the rent and the price paid only reflect the profit made by the grantor. Often other rents would be payable as well. In the example given on p.45, for example, James and Marion have not only to pay the root of ginger to the grantors, William and Katerina, but also 26d to the lords of the fee. For this reason, the rent paid by a tenant for years or at will is more likely to be an accurate reflection of the value of the property, as in this case the lessor would continue to pay the rent due to the lords of the fee himself. To take this same example: had William and Katerina wished to make a profit of 6s on the grant of their messuage they could have reserved a rent of 6s. Had they been leasing it for years or at will, on the other hand, they would have had to charge a rent of 8s 2d to cover the 26d payable to the lords of the fee in order to make the same profit. In this example the difference between the rents is not very great. Had, however, there been due from the messuage the, by no means unusual, rent of 7s, which was paid from a stall granted by a deed enrolled in January 1288[91] (2s to the city and 5s to the Great Hospital), then the difference would be between an assize rent of 6s and a leasehold rent of 13s. Such pre-existing rents suggest one possible reason why mainly nominal rents were being reserved between 1285 and 1290. As a result of frequent subinfeudation during the 13th century, some properties may already have been paying out in rents almost as much as they were worth, making it impossible for a grantor to reserve more than a nominal rent.

d) RAISING THE MONEY

Mention has already been made of quitclaims which released rights in property back to a former owner (p.53)) and grants could be used for the same purpose. The object of such a grant or quitclaim may not have been just to simplify the tenurial situation or to conform with any right of pre-emption held by the lord.[92] Instead, these may have been properties formerly granted as security for loans and now redeemed. If so, the number of such mortgages was never very great. To the few (under ten for either period) regrants and quitclaims enrolled might be added a complicated transaction involving Yizhannus de Hedersete and his brother. By a grant enrolled in July 1287, John de Eton transferred to Yizhannus his capital messuage and other properties and goods for £40. Yizhannus transferred them all to his brother Alan de Hedersete, and Alan regranted them to John de Eton for £42 by a deed enrolled in August 1287.[93] The amount paid on the regrant may include a concealed payment of interest. There is also one case where a deed was delivered by Hugh de Kyrkeby and Joan, his wife, to the bailiff, on condition that it only be delivered to the grantee if Hugh and Joan fail to pay him £20 within the next few months.[94] A quick look through the computer index to the rolls from G to O inclusive failed to reveal more than one grant and regrant over a longer period. This was of a stall granted by deed enrolled in 1290 by Robert Candelarius and Christiana, his wife, to Adam de Saham, which was regranted by a deed enrolled in November 1299.[95] The explanation for such a small number of possible mortgages might be that leases for years were more commonly employed than grants for this purpose, but were not enrolled, as they did not concern freehold interests. Another possible explanation, however, is that it was customary to raise money in Norwich by the use of rent charges, a method which affected neither the ownership nor the possession of the property concerned. It has already been mentioned that grants could convey rents which had originated either as reserved rents or as rents charged by the holder on property in favour of someone else (see p.51). There are, however, many grants where the terminology used suggests that the grantor of the rent was in current occupation of the property from which the rent was to be paid.[96] To give just two examples, in October 1285 Roger, son of Adam, son of Gilbert, of Norwich, granted a 12d rent from his capital messuage (de capitali mesuagio predicti Rogeri), and in November 1285 Geoffrey de Eston and Matilda, his wife, granted a 6s rent out of their messuage (de mesuagio predictorum Galfridi et Matildis).[97] In such cases the transaction enrolled appears to be not the transfer of a pre-existing rent, but the creation of a new rentcharge on the grantor's property. Although the wording is often ambiguous, this could be so in all of the grants, forty-six (57.5%) for 1285-90 and thirty-four (62%) for 1306-11, where no one other than the grantor is described as holding the property from which the rent, or part of the rent, granted is to be paid. Such rentcharges could be created for a variety of different purposes. They could be used to provide for a member of the family, as when, by a deed enrolled in September 1287, Matilda granted to her father, William de Welles, a rent of 11s for his life,[98] or to make up the value in an exchange of properties, as in the example on p.45. Their main use, however, was probably to raise money. As an alternative to a mortgage of tenements, this had the great advantage that neither ownership nor the right to occupation need change hands, and if necessary more money could always be raised by the same means. By a deed enrolled in 1287, for example, Guy le Chapeller and Cecilia, his wife, granted to Thomas Godesman and Margaret, his wife, a 12d rent out of their messuage, with the right to distrain not only for this rent, but also for another 7s owed to Thomas and Margaret out of the same messuage.[99] There is no significant difference between the value of rentcharges apparently created in this way and the value of other rents conveyed.

This ability to raise money by the creation of a rentcharge may have had an affect on the composition of the property-holding class in Norwich at this date. The shift from paying primarily for property by a rentservice reserved to the grantor to paying by a lump sum, which the high proportion of nominal rents reserved 1285-90 implies, meant that a purchase price which hitherto would have been found out of income now had to be found out of capital. As a result of rents already payable out of a property, the lump sum required in the mid-13th century need not have been very high, but, by the 14th century, either because of increasing property values, or because some of the rents payable had been extinguished, the gap between the amount to be paid out of a tenement in rents and its annual value is likely to have widened. One means of raising the lump sum to fill this gap might be by raising a rentcharge on a newly purchased property in favour of a third party. In this way it would again become possible to raise a purchase price out of income rather than out of capital, thus making ownership of property available to a wider section of the community. There are two occasions on the rolls 1285-90 where this appears to be happening.[100] It is perhaps not surprising that there are not more examples even if this was a common practice. It will only be obvious from the rolls where both the purchase of property and the creation of a rentcharge are enrolled, and where they are enrolled together. In addition, both pre-existing rents and new rent charges could themselves be mortgaged. During 1285-90 the rolls include four grants of rents coupled with separate agreements that they should be returned if (in three cases), money was paid within a specified time or (in the fourth case), if a debt due to the Exchequer from a messuage sold by the grantor to the grantee was paid.[101] A final method of financing a purchase was by granting another property in exchange (in escambium) as in the example on p.45. The numbers of these were very small - under ten for both periods together.

e) EXTENT OF OWNER-OCCUPATION

It is important to realise that not all the holders of property given in the court rolls would necessarily have been in occupation of the property they held. The rolls are only concerned with freehold interests, and give no information about lessees for years or tenants at will. A late 13th-century survey of the northern half of King's Lynn, for instance, shows considerable evidence of non-occupation by the holder of the freehold.[102] Ten men each held five or more messuages there at the date of the survey, and one John Costin held no fewer than thirty-four properties at once. Two factors, however, may point to a fairly high level of occupation by the owner of the freehold. One is the continuing creation, by the city and the prior of Norwich among others, of demises for life and at fee farm as a source of income. Even if all such deeds are not enrolled, tenants for life and at fee farm had freehold interests, and should therefore appear as the holders of abuttals in the rolls. Secondly, the ability to raise the purchase price of property by means of a rentcharge meant that payment could be made out of income rather than out of capital. This, while of course dependent on the level of income (and not making property ownership possible for all), must nevertheless have made it more widely available.

f) CONCLUSION

The statute of Quia Emptores in 1290 appears to have had little practical effect. Many nominal and symbolic rents were reserved on grants before the statute, and it is these rents that are so much reduced in number by 1306. Higher rents continued to be reserved as before despite the abolition of subinfeudation. In view of the continued creation of freehold rents by institutions, and at least one individual with extensive interests in property, it seems likely that the largely nominal rents reserved before 1290 were not the result of a swing by investors towards leasing for years or at will. The explanation is more likely to be found in the low transfer value of properties already paying high rents of assize as a result of frequent subinfeudation, or in the ready availability of the money needed to pay for property by a lump sum. One possible way of acquiring this money was by charging property with a rentcharge. This appears to have been the normal method of raising money, and the number of explicit or implicit mortgages enrolled is very small. The possibility of raising money in this way, and therefore paying the purchase price out of income, may have encouraged occupation by the owner of the freehold in Norwich at this period.

THE ENROLLED DEEDS AS SOURCE MATERIAL

Any view of late 13th and early 14th-century Norwich drawn from the city court rolls must necessarily be a partial one. In the first place, only deeds concerning freehold interests in land were entered on the rolls. This meant that, not only is that part of the population of Norwich living in lodgings or hiring dwellings as tenants at will entirely absent from the rolls, but even those who held tenements under lease for a stated term of years rarely appear. Moreover, at no period were even all deeds relating to freehold interests enrolled. Also, though the names of most freeholders of neighbouring properties are known from the descriptions given in the deeds, their occupation and status may not be recorded, as this information is usually only included for the parties of the deeds enrolled. In the 14th century, when it became usual to enrol joint deeds by husbands and wives to defeat possible future claims to dower, the rolls probably contain details of a wide cross-section of the Norwich landowning community, and it may be that most grants made by married men were enrolled at this period. In the 13th century, however, when the rolls are being used for less specialised purposes, there is probably a decided bias in favour of the more wealthy members of the community, as they are most likely to have undertaken the trouble and expense of enrolment.

Not all parties to deeds, of course, were necessarily in occupation of the properties in which they held an interest. Apart from the possibility that some owners let their property to tenants for years or at will, others were not, and never had been, in a position to occupy the property concerned. Obvious examples are the recipients of newly created rentcharges, and often both the grantors and purchasers of pre-existing rents. Once again, this is less of a problem in the 14th-century rolls. Nearly a quarter of all parties to the deeds enrolled 1285-90 were not, and never had been, holders of the property concerned, but by 1306-11 the proportion of non-holders had dropped to less than a sixth. On the other hand, most of the grants enrolled are probably genuine sales, as there are few apparent mortgages or re-allocations of family interest, and so the rolls should given an accurate picture of freehold property holding in Norwich.

Some of the detailed information given in the enrolments must also be used with caution. The date of enrolment, for instance, need not be the date of transaction, and the apparently common practice of creating rentcharges out of one's own property could make the rents payable a very uncertain guide either to house values or to previous holders of the property. Even the amount paid from a tenement in landgable, which might reasonably be expected to be a fixed rent, could be increased, as is shown by the enrolled licences to encroach on waste.

Finally, interpretation of the evidence may be affected by the legal background. It would be wrong, for instance, to assume from the many enrolled grants made jointly by husbands and wives that it was customary for Norwich wives to hold property jointly with their husbands, when often the wives appear to have been joined as parties to the deeds simply to bar any future claim to dower. It might also be worth considering how far the extensive subdivision of Norwich properties shown by many of the reconstructions was due to partible inheritance (sharing of property between all sons, or all children) as well as to economic factors.

ENDNOTES

1. Norfolk Record Office (hereafter NRO), Norwich City Records, case 1, shelf a, Court Rolls 1-5. (Hereafter, references to the court rolls will give roll and membrane numbers only.)

2. NRO, Norwich City Records, Private Deeds (hereafter PD), case 4.

3. NRO, Dean and Chapter Records, Norwich Deeds (hereafter DC).

4. The Norwich City Court rolls are by no means an unknown source. Extensive extracts, especially from the two late-13th-century rolls, were printed in W.Hudson and J.C.Tingey (eds.), The Records of the City of Norwich (Norwich 1906 and 1910); W.Rye published two brief calendars of the deeds enrolled 1285-1341, giving the parties and the parish in which the property involved lay, in A short calendar of deeds relating to Norwich enrolled in the court rolls of that city 1285-1306, (Norwich 1903), and Calendar of Norwich deeds enrolled in the court rolls of that city 1307-1341, (Norwich 1915); while a list of the wills proved in the city court, 1286-1508, is included in Part III of M.A.Farrow (ed.), Wills at Norwich, 1370-1550 (Norfolk Record Society 16, 1943-45).

5. G.H.Martin, The Early Court Rolls of the Borough of Ipswich (University College of Leicester, Department of English Local History, Occasional Paper 5, 1954), p.33.

6. PD, St Peter Mancroft, 1250-59.

7. G.H.Martin, 'The English Borough in the Thirteenth Century', Transactions of the Royal Historical Society 5th series 13, 1963, pp.137-8; Martin, Early Court Rolls of ... Ipswich, p.27.

8. Hudson and Tingey state that earlier rolls are mentioned but lost. Tantalisingly they give no references. Records of ... Norwich I, p.xxxiii.

9. Martin, Early Court Rolls of ... Ipswich, p.26; P.Rutledge, Handlist of the Archives of Great Yarmouth Corporation (Cyclostyled n.d.), p.7.

10. Hudson and Tingey, Records of ... Norwich I and II, passim.

11. Roll 5, m.28d. (references to the dorse of a membrane are qualified by 'd').

12. Roll 5, m.12.

13. Hudson and Tingey, Records of ... Norwich II, pp.29-30.

14. Martin, Early Court Rolls of ... Ipswich, pp.16 and 27.

15. e.g. Hudson and Tingey, Records of ... Norwich I, p.164.

16. Roll 1, m.2.

17. G.H.Martin (ed.), The Ipswich Recognizance Rolls, 1294-1327 (Suffolk Record Society 16, 1973), passim.

18. Roll 1, m.3; Roll 2, m.20.

19. e.g. Hudson and Tingey, Records of ... Norwich I, pp.161 and 164.

20. See e.g. Roll 2, m.30.

21. Hudson and Tingey, Records of ... Norwich I, p.xxv and passim.

22. PD, St Peter Mancroft, 1240-1377.

23. DC, St Peter Mancroft, box 30.

24. Such as those discussed above, p.19.

25. H.Le Strange, Norfolk Official Lists (Norwich 1890), p.129.

26. PD, St Peter Mancroft, 1290-99.

27. PD and DC, St Peter Mancroft.

28. Hudson and Tingey, Records of ... Norwich I, pp.170-4.

29. Roll 2, m.19.

30. Roll 5, m.28.

31. M.Bateson (ed.), Borough Customs (Selden Society 18 and 21, 1899 and 1905), I, pp.273-4.

32. PD, St Peter Mancroft, 1270-79.

33. Hudson and Tingey, Records of ... Norwich I, pp.163-4.

34. Roll 2, m.9d; Hudson and Tingey, Records of ... Norwich II, p.7 no.XI.

35. Bateson, Borough Customs I, p.274.

36. Roll 5, m.20; Roll 1, m.3; Hudson and Tingey, Records of ... Norwich I, p.231 no. CII.

37. By the time the custumal appears again in a 15th-century copy in the Book of Pleas, these charges have been raised to 4d and 2s respectively; Hudson and Tingey, Records of ... Norwich I, pp.cxxii and 164.

38. Bateson, Borough Customs I, p.271; Martin, Ipswich Recognizance Rolls, passim.

39. A grant by Nicholas de Ingham and Gundreda his wife was enrolled 13 December, 1285, and disputed 23 December, 1286; Roll 1, m.1d. See Bateson, Borough Customs I, pp.274-5.

40. Membrane 35 from Roll 4, for instance, should come between membranes 24 and 25, and two entries on Roll 1, membrane 3, which chronologically should be near the end of the membrane, have been squeezed into a gap left earlier on.

41. PD, boxes 6 and 8; DC, St Peter Mancroft.

42. PD, St Peter Mancroft, 1280-89.

43. Roll 2, m.16; Hudson and Tingey, Records of ... Norwich I, p.226 no.XCI.

44. Roll 5, m.31.

45. Roll 1, m.3.

46. Roll 2, m.8d.

47. Roll 1, m.3.

48. Roll 2, m.19.

49. Roll 5, m.11.

50. Roll 2, m.4.

51. 40% in 1285-90 and 33% in 1306-11.

52. See, for example, Roll 2, m.31d, for a reference in a grant by Roger de Rokhawe and Alice his wife to a division between the son and daughter of William de Knapeton. Partible inheritance was probably very general in boroughs. Borough English, where property was inherited by the youngest son, was not such a characteristic borough custom as its name implies. Bateson, Borough Customs II, p.xcv.

53. Hudson and Tingey, Records of ... Norwich I, pp.162-3.

54. There is only one example, on Roll 5, m.10.

55. See e.g. deed by Roger de Tybenham, Roll 2, m.27d.

56. Hudson and Tingey, Records of ... Norwich I, pp.156 and 158-60.

57. Bateson, Borough Customs II, p.cxxxviii.

58. Will of Roger de Tudenham. PD, St Peter Mancroft, 1300-1310.

59. William de Burtoft, James Nade, John de Poringland, Thomas de Shaftesbury, Roger de Tudenham. 42 out of 146.

60. Hudson and Tingey, Records of ... Norwich I, pp.163-4.

61. Roll 2, m.21.

62. Hudson and Tingey, Records of ... Norwich I, pp.147-8.

63. Bateson, Borough Customs II, p.ci onwards.

64. Chapter 25 of the custumal only refers to conveyance of property acquired jointly by a husband and wife, but, as endorsement and enrolment in the city court are said to have the force of a fine in the king's courts, any property held by the wife before her marriage could presumably be transferred in the same way.

65. Hudson and Tingey, Records of ... Norwich I, pp.154-5.

66. The grant of Newgate actually had little effect on the rolls. The number of deeds enrolled transferring property within the parish of St Stephen, in which Newgate lay, fell between 1285-90 and 1306-11 from 34 to 24.

67. Entries for 1296 begin on Roll 2,m.50, which also covers part of November and December of the preceding year; the change to m.51 comes in the middle of the March entries and that to m.52 in the middle of the May entries; the remaining entries for 1296 are all on m.52 which also contains enrolments for the following January and February.

68. PD, St Peter Mancroft. The Nedlerowe agreements have not been included.

69. These are grants where the former husband, father or other relation of the wife is described as a former owner, or where the wife is described as the widow or daughter of a named person. The numbers are percentages of different totals.

70. Hudson and Tingey, Records of ... Norwich I, p.xxxix.

71. Bateson, Borough Customs II, p.cxxxviii, see above p.54.

72. See e.g. Martin, Ipswich Recognizance Rolls, p.10.

73. Roll 5, m.23d.

74. The enrolments for 1285-90 include one rent of 8s 8d reserved on a demise for life and three rents of 10s each reserved at fee farm; those for 1306-11 include one rent of 20s reserved on a demise for life and rents of 9s,10s, 10s and 12s reserved on four demises at fee farm.

75. See e.g. A.W.B.Simpson, An introduction to the History of Land Law (London 1964), p.74 as against pp.51 and 53.

76. A quitclaim of rights in a messuage acquired for a term of years. Roll 5, m.8d.

77. Account roll of Peter Flynt, 1293-1306. NRO, Norwich City Records, case 7 shelf a; Hudson and Tingey, Records of ... Norwich II, p.30 onwards.

78. Hudson and Tingey, Records of ... Norwich II, pp.209-212.

79. PD, St Peter Mancroft, 1290-99.

80. See the account of Hervy de Stanho, Custos of Norwich, 1272-3: Hudson and Tingey, Records of ... Norwich II, pp.404-5 no.CCCCLXXI.

81. Roll 2, mm.28,30,33 and 33d.

82. PD, St Peter Mancroft, 1300-1310.

83. H.W. Saunders, An Introduction to the Obedientary and Manor Rolls of Norwich Cathedral Priory (Norwich 1930), passim.

84. DC, Obedientary rolls nos. 113,120,486 and 491.

85. DC, Obedientary rolls nos. 113 and 120.

86. DC, Obedientary roll no.491.

87. Roll 2, m.30d; DC, St Peter Mancroft, box 30, no.2150.

88. Roll 2, m.59d.

89. Roll 2, mm.14,17,18d and 23.

90. For their holdings see above, pp.21-22.

91. Roll 2, m.9d.

92. In some boroughs a lord had the right of first refusal to a tenement offered for sale.

93. Roll 2, mm.3d and 4.

94. Roll 5, m.29.

95. Rolls 2, m.26d, and 3, m.5d.

96. The existence of this practice is indirectly supported by Chapter 32 of the custumal which begins 'Also in a case where a man sells a rent of assize in the city issuing out of a tenement in another's tenancy than his own...' Hudson and Tingey, Records of ... Norwich I, pp.170-1.

97. Both on Roll 1, m.1.

98. Roll 2, m.4d.

99. Roll 1, m.2d.

100. Roll 2, mm.2 and 25. This point illustrates one of the problems in using the court rolls. Did the two transactions take place at the same time or was the property purchased earlier and the sale only enrolled later because the purchaser of the rentcharge wanted better security?

101. Rolls 1, m.1, and 2, mm.8,9 and 18.

102. See E. and P.Rutledge, 'King's Lynn and Great Yarmouth, two thirteenth-century surveys', Norfolk Archaeology XXXVII, 1978, pp.92-114.

Fig. 2

Fold-out opposite to be read with pp. 5-10 above.

Reconstruction of the Norwich Blackfriars site *c.* 1310-1325. The handwritten entries record information obtained from the St Andrew's Private Deeds, e.g. (P.D.2), and the City court rolls, e.g. (2.52d).

Overprinted in red is the outline of the friars' church, together with the dimensions derived from Kirkpatrick's *History of the Religious Orders ....*

See footnotes 1-3 on p.11 for further details of the references.

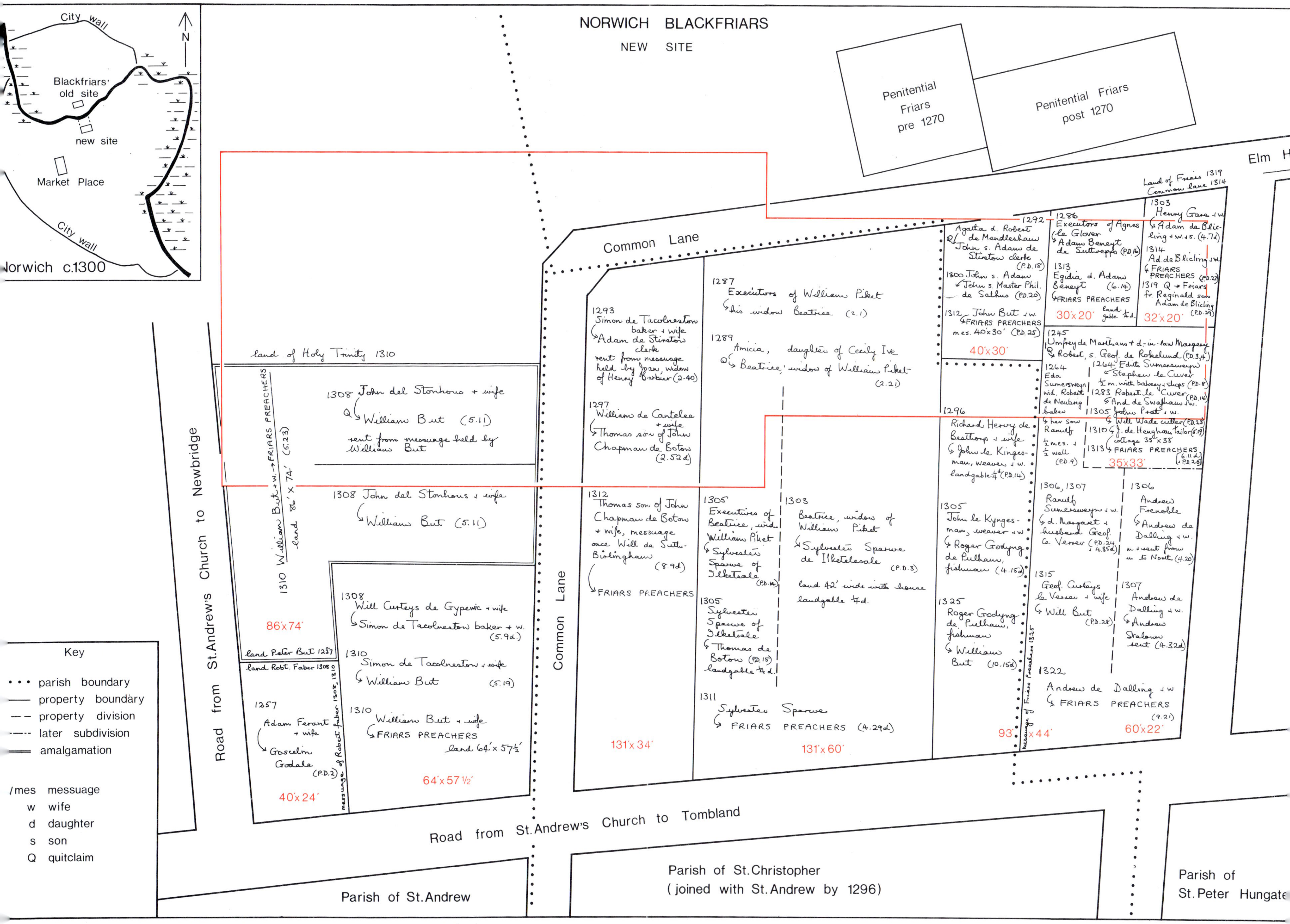
NORWICH BLACKFRIARS
NEW SITE
Penitential Friars pre 1270
Penitential Friars post 1270
Elm Hill
Common Lane
Common Lane
Road from St.Andrew's Church to Newbridge
Road from St.Andrew's Church to Tombland
Parish of St.Andrew
Parish of St.Christopher
(joined with St.Andrew by 1296)
Parish of St.Peter Hungate
City wall
Blackfriars' old site
new site
Market Place
City wall
Norwich c.1300
N
Key
parish boundary
property boundary
property division
later subdivision
amalgamation
/mes message
w wife
d daughter
s son
Q quitclaim
86'x74'
40'x24'
64'x57½'
131'x34'
131'x60'
40'x30'
30'x20'
32'x20'
35'x33'
93'x44'
60'x22'